MW01633243

Praise

Andy's journey from a skinny teen to a competitive bodybuilder is a powerful example of how focusing on fitness can elevate confidence and fuel personal growth. His story reveals how discipline and commitment can transform not only your body but also your life. I am both inspired and impressed by his example.

Bruce Salomon | Founder and Chief Investment Officer, Elberon Investment Fund

This book also serves as parental advice as it emphasizes the importance of teaching children values like confidence and initiative, which can shape their success for generations to come.

Greg Stock | Chairman & CEO, Zenoss, Inc.

I know Andy Allen personally. To meet Andy is to meet a man who is obviously focused, disciplined, happy and successful. What he shares in *The 80 Percent Project* is what he is living. In this book, he teaches us how to live it too. Thank you Andy.

Dr. Will Davis Jr. | Founding and Sr. Pastor, Austin Christian Fellowship

There has never been a book that breaks down the blueprint for success as perfectly as Andy does in *The 80 Percent Project*. Finally, someone is showing that having it all isn't just something to strive for—it's truly possible to achieve. Andy's approach embraces an intentional imbalance in favor of life, proving that success doesn't have to come at the expense of living fully.

Danielle Garofalo | Founder, CEO, Think Billion Dollar

This book is very inspiring! I love how it emphasizes living life with purpose and intention - truly working to live. Andy Allen's advice about prioritizing time, staying disciplined, and finding motivation really will hit home for a lot of people. I love the idea of tackling the hardest things first and staying competitive.. it's a powerful reminder to push yourself. Most of all, focusing on living intentionally to leave a legacy for family later is so meaningful. Definitely relatable and a motivating read!

Sage Northcutt | Professional Athlete, MMA

This book reminds us that you don't have to sacrifice everything to succeed—you can have a life full of purpose.

Bob Mitchell | Personal Trainer/Triathlete

The 80 Percent Project is the blueprint to living an amazing life! Andy has presented us with a clear plan to being truly successful, not just financially or professionally, but achieving whole life success. I only wish I'd learned the principles in this book 20 years ago. If you want to live an unimaginable life, reading this book is a great first step in the right direction!

Brad Mullen | Serial Entrepreneur and Investor

THE
80 PERCENT
PROJECT

UNLOCK EXCEPTIONAL RESULTS.
LIVE AN UNIMAGINABLE LIFE.
CREATE GENERATIONAL CHANGE.

ANDY ALLEN

ISBN **978-1-63735-359-2** (pbk)

ISBN **978-1-63735-360-8** (hcv)

ISBN **978-1-63735-358-5** (ebook)

Library of Congress Control Number: **2024922922**

Dedication

For the 2 heroes in my life, my beautiful wife, Janiene and my less beautiful but equally important dad, Retired U.S. Army Colonel Carl Allen (aka Pop).

Preface

I've lived an unimaginable life…one I had previously believed was reserved for action heroes and sports superstars. Now it's time for me to share how I did it, in hopes you can start experiencing your own unimaginable lives. To illustrate the value of living with a Life Pie and being intentional about the things you believe to be most important in your life (not just work), I've shared many stories of my family's life so you can see the changes that will be coming for your family. I was fortunate to have been taught this early in my career, and my kids grew up with it, learning through osmosis, but after reading this book, you will understand the profound impact small, intentional effort will make in the most important areas of your own lives. By making these purposeful changes, you will not just be teaching your children, but you will also be making a much larger change that affects generations to come. The 80 Percenters that I've coached have been amazed by the immediate improvements that occur in their lives with such little effort. It's my hope that this book, and the stories it tells, will clearly show you what you've been missing. You deserve to live your best life, and I'm excited to show you how.

Acknowledgements

Thanks to Gary Keller, who taught me work is only to support your unimaginable life.

Thanks to Danielle Garofalo, marketing Guru, and her star pupil, Kailey Greilich, for pushing me to write this book.

Thanks to Phoenix Roberts, my writing coach.

Thanks to my wife and my kids for letting me share so many of our stories. I'm incredibly proud of all of you!!

Thanks to my mom and dad for raising me to believe anything is possible and for showing our family what true love looks like.

And thanks to everyone who reads this book. I hope you allow me to return the favor by focusing on your other 80 percent and allowing yourself to live your unimaginable life.

Table of Contents

CHAPTER 1

Success is Intentional

I live an unimaginable life. In the pages of this book, I will show you how to live one too.

Success is intentional, not just in business, but in every aspect of your life. Not paying attention to the other parts of your life is also intentional. By not choosing to pay attention to other aspects, you're also making a choice. People are good with that; professional success (in academia or business or some industry or another) is all that matters.

If you're one of those people, you probably think this book is not for you. But I believe you need it more than anyone else—and it can be life-changing. If I give you the step-by-step process to truly create and live your unimaginable life, and you take no action, that will be intentional.

Throughout my career, some of the unhappiest people I've worked with have also been some of the wealthiest. They sacrificed family time, community involvement, and even their mental and physical health for success, believing that those sacrifices were necessary to become successful. I'm not saying you can "have it all"—nobody gets through life without bad days. However, if you are open to learning a better way, you can have so much in so many areas of life, that you won't be devastated when your business life faces challenges.

It's never too late to make minor changes that will create huge differences. If you're truly driven, welcome to a new reality—one where you're more efficient in your work life because you're also focused on enjoying the other aspects of your life. Study this book, and you'll understand that the life you lead along the way is as important as the result you're chasing. Some of us were lucky enough to learn this from our parents. For those of you who weren't so lucky, I've written this book.

I consider myself incredibly fortunate because, early in life, at home with my parents, I was taught principles that work. As I started to experience some success, I was mentored by some amazing people who knew how to create a more broad-based success. After years of following good advice from people who didn't just know it, but also lived it, I'm an example of *The 80 Percent Project*. I've enjoyed exceptional results in my work, among my family, and elsewhere. I've achieved a life that, as a child, I thought was unimaginable. My wife and I have created generational change by helping our children understand that high-level success is possible while living an amazing life.

My goal in writing this book remains simple: to teach people that achieving a remarkably elevated level doesn't require sacrificing your family relationships, health, personal time, or other things. Acting with intention, life can be amazing along the way to whatever success you envision. You simply have to buy into four foundational ideas:

1.   Stop what you're doing right now.
2.   Know that this is possible.
3.   Give yourself the chance to be led in a new direction.
4.   Embrace the process.

Let's Start near the Beginning

The Lessons

The Calendar

I've been a real estate agent for over 30 years. When I first broke into the top twenty agents in the country, I was invited to join Keller-Williams mastermind meetings. I believe the first I attended was in Las Vegas, and I remember that we were told to bring our calendars. I walked into the room where several tables were set up in a horseshoe. That image is still fresh in my mind because it was a little bit intimidating to show up to a meeting of top agents who had already been together for some time. They were significantly older than me, and they'd all brought their calendars–paper ones back then. Nineteen other agents and me sitting around the tables.

In walks Gary Keller–founder and chief of Keller-Williams, the biggest real estate agency in the world. Right off the bat, he told us to pull out our calendars. Then, he told us to start filling in every vacation we wanted to take over the course of the next year.

I'm sitting there, looking around and I'm thinking, "I've never heard of anything like this. Why would anybody be writing down every vacation they wanted to take? This was supposed to be about work, right?" But it's my first time as part of the group, so, I'm watching as everyone around me writes and turns the page then writes more and turns the next page.

I thought, "All right, well, I'll buy in." Mostly, I didn't want to question what everyone was doing on my very first day there, so, I went ahead and filled in my calendar, all the while thinking, "He's got to be kidding!" But I look around and everyone else is still feverishly writing all over their calendars, so I did the same.

Next, he told us to write down all the date nights we wanted with our spouses, any events we wanted to attend, trips to visit parents, all the kids' events—practices, games, recitals, birthday parties—everything! He concluded by telling us that anything he'd left out, fill it in now.

Gary then explained: The rest of our time—the unmarked, unreserved time—we were to work to support that "perfect life" we'd just documented for ourselves.

This whole theory was incredibly foreign to me but, somehow, it made perfect sense. Family and personal time first, then work to support your life. Why had I never heard this before? It was so simple. I didn't even know I was allowed to think this way, but I've never thought any other way since.

The Mindset

Speaking of not knowing I could think that way: At that first mastermind meeting, I had what I thought was a clever idea. These were the top-performing agents in the Keller-Williams system, so at the end of our few days together, I suggested a little friendly competition: Each agent would put a certain amount of money into a pot. We'd post our sales numbers regularly and, one year later, the agent with the biggest increase (in gross sales or percentage or whatever measure they chose) would take home the pot. Because of my competitive nature (intentionally understated to make me look better), this would be a huge motivation for the coming year. Plus, I knew being able to watch others' sales would only drive my production higher.

They all looked at me like I had two heads! A competition like this seemed inconceivable to them. I got this look of disgust like they were thinking, "How in the world did this guy get in the room?" It really struck me as odd; how could these successful people not want to be pushed to do more? Because I'd competed in sports my entire life, including as a bodybuilder in college and after, it was natural for me. To them, it was not—they had experienced similar levels of success, but clearly followed a different path to get there.

This, too, has stuck with me. Now, these were KW's most successful agents, so I understand that each of them had a system that worked for them. I wasn't suggesting they change their system; I suggested they add a little incentive to what they already did.

Not one of them signed on. They were all extraordinarily successful and, just maybe, they all decided that they couldn't change what worked.

An Unexpected Example

One of the things Gary mentioned was time with parents. I feel I was truly blessed with my parents, so time with them has been a priority as they have gotten older. With the goal of living a life with no regrets, and knowing they can't live forever, I've made the drive from Austin to San Antonio to visit them every Thursday for the last eight years. My mom passed away from Alzheimer's two years ago, but my trips to visit her, especially the last year when she was in a wheelchair and could no longer put her words together to make sentences, have left me with amazing memories. Seeing her face light up when I would get there, playing her favorite music for her from my phone, and helping her from her chair so we could dance to *The Twist* by Chubby Checker, are all memories that I would never have if I hadn't been intentional about spending time with my parents.

Thursdays still include my trip to San Antonio to see Dad and visit Mom at the cemetery. I leave my Austin home at 6:30 a.m., so Dad and I can meet at the same restaurant every Thursday at eight. We sit at the same table and almost always have the same waitress, Kathy.

She's about my age, I'm guessing, and she loves to travel. Several times a year, she's gone on a trip or a cruise to an island here or there. It's clear that Kathy only works to support her real life. She never got the "pull out your calendar" speech., She figured it out entirely on her own. And

I can't tell you how impressed I am by that, especially knowing so many highly successful people who never figured it out on their own. I've even told her how I love that she works to live, rather than living to work.

So many have not figured it out. They're the ones for whom everything revolves around their work. In truth, everything you do should be exactly the opposite. As Dad and I catch up on the week's adventures, Kathy will tell us, "Oh, yeah, I'm going here or there next month," and she does. Then, she's back, picking up a few extra shifts to make the money she needs for her next adventure. It is exactly what Gary tried to teach us, and what he (fortunately!) did teach me at that early age. When Gary said, "God, family, work," my entire life changed, my business life and personal life, because I was given permission to live the life I felt called to live. I still get out my calendar. I still put in my family time—all I want— and I now work during other hours to support that life.

My family has done lots of cruises, beach trips, mountain trips, and every other kind of vacation that sounded like fun. Virtually every year, my family would have a couple of vacations. In addition, I coached all the kids' sports—every sport they wanted to take part in, I coached them and their team.

How Do I Make it Work?

Most people know that real estate, as an industry, has no ceiling and can be very lucrative for those few who figure out what it takes and do the work to make it happen. That's one reason why so many people make a pass through my industry. Sadly, many of those who achieve success end up having little or no life outside work. In real estate, as in many other sales industries, the better the sales, the more money you make. So, if you're motivated "to be successful"—that is, "to make lots of money"—you push yourself by working more hours.

Now, if I'm helping you find a home and you work in an office or factory, you may have a few minutes free at seven or eight o'clock in the morning, so, you might shoot me a quick text, saying, "Hey, about the houses we saw, I'm thinking of doing this and that," or, "This just popped up, can you check it for me?"

Of course, I can. But I can't do anything with that info because you're likely at work and can't leave to see the house even if I think it's a great fit. Most people see houses on Saturdays or Sundays. In summer, they can also go after work because it's still light at 8:00 p.m. or 9:00 p.m. It's not unusual, then, that I could be out in the evenings until nine. I don't get home until around half past nine—meaning there's just time to grab a quick bite, go to bed, and start it all again the next day.

This is how people in my industry can, even if they're successful, get wildly overwhelmed because they believe they need to be ready for those early emails at seven o'clock in the morning and work showing houses straight through until nine at night.

People think, "I'll just hit Andy up with a quick question." Some days, I do get text messages at seven o'clock in the morning and they continue coming until ten at night. That doesn't mean I have to immediately act on that question. If I didn't prioritize my time and my family time, I would likely have had a short-lived career in real estate, cranking out big sales until I couldn't take another day.

This is my "80-percent" mindset. I think of my life as a pie with five pieces—details to follow—but the eight years of trips to see my parents came as a result of that Life Pie. Work is one slice of that pie, 20 percent, but I've carved out time to do other important things—the 80 percent. I do them without regret or guilt.

Suppose a client says, "Hey Andy, man, I'd like to look at these two houses. How about tomorrow evening?"

I might respond, "Let me check. Yeah, that's not going to work. I'm solidly booked tomorrow evening, but I could do the day after. Or, if you want to meet at lunch tomorrow, we could knock out a viewing or two."

I serve my clients on an equal level with my family. My wife and kids understand that I sometimes have a business thing I must attend. On the flip side, if a client calls and I've booked a family thing, there's nothing that says I have to tell the client why I'm booked.

But—and this is the key—I am indeed **booked**. My calendar says I have a previously scheduled engagement, such as coaching Little League. I made a promise and I'm going to keep it. This mindset allows me to be off work on the baseball field at four in the afternoon with a clear conscience. I question whether most agents know that they're allowed to work this way. My coaching with Gary taught me that my time and my family time are also important.

Now, you're thinking, "Well, this is real estate. In the end, you're all independent; your own bosses."

True, but being intentional with **all** aspects of your life is important for all of us. Exceptional results, an unimaginable life, and generational change are attainable for those who are driven, and this book will show you how.

Discipline

Discipline is trading what you want now for what you want most.

Discipline makes all this work. Discipline isn't the only factor, as subsequent chapters will describe, and it isn't natural to some people. Even so, it has to be learned (and can be) if you want to achieve a high level, and especially if you want to have an amazing, purposeful life while achieving that success.

For me, the discipline required in bodybuilding helped set the stage for success in my business endeavors. Once developed, discipline translates to all parts of your life. It is what allows you to stay on track with your Life Pie. While you might expect that this would be obvious, for most people, it isn't. Most don't really understand what is possible for them because they lack the discipline to achieve at a higher level.

Bodybuilding

My family moved to San Antonio, Texas, for my junior year of high school. The first kid I met was a tennis player. Before that, I'd played baseball, basketball, and football for years. My dad went through college on a basketball scholarship, so my brother and I were blessed with excellent sports genes. Well, I don't know much about tennis, so I got a tennis racket, and my new friend and I started playing tennis every day. Seriously, that summer, we sometimes played some days for eight hours. I got good quickly and decided to play tennis at my new school.

At that time, I didn't understand that tennis was a year-round sport. Every other sport I'd played had a season and I played several sports throughout the year. So, in my ignorance, I tried out, made varsity, and competed with the team. By the Christmas break, I'm thinking, "Oh man, I'm so burnt out on this damn tennis. I can't wait for baseball." That was when I learned that the tennis team competes year-round. I immediately went to my dad and told him I'm going to quit tennis to play baseball. His answer was simple. "You committed, so, you're not going to quit tennis; you're going to keep playing." And, so, there I was, stuck on the tennis court until the end of that school year, by which time, I was totally over tennis!

Now, I grew up in the 1970s and, in the back of about every comic book ever printed were ads featuring a skinny guy getting sand kicked in his face by some big bully. The skinny guy finds an ad for Charles Atlas (the Arnold Schwarzenegger of that decade) and takes up bodybuilding. He then goes back to the beach, kicks sand in the face of the bully, and gets the girl.

At age 16, I was five foot eleven inches tall and weighed 135 pounds. I was that skinny kid, and I decided to change. Fortunately for me, another guy I met when I first moved to San Antonio was a lifter. He'd come over to my garage and show me how to work out and it didn't take long for me to notice a change.

"Wow," I thought, "I can see, and other people can see, the changes in me from working out." Lifting became my priority. There were even days when I'd sneak out of tennis practice and go to the gym. By the beginning of my senior year, I was beginning to look a little more like Charles Atlas. Then, as soon as I was out of high school, my focus became the gym.

Within ten years, the skinny sixteen-year-old kid had added one inch in height and almost doubled his body weight to 262 pounds. That doesn't just happen. It's created by discipline. You never miss workouts. During college, I was a bouncer for a year and a half. I'd get off work at 2:30 a.m., grab a bite to eat, then go to the gym. In the 1980s, you should know, there were no 24-hour gyms. So, wherever I worked out, I'd get to know the owner so well that they'd give me a key. So, I'd go in at four in the morning and train for two hours. I'd be home by six to start school and sleep all afternoon. That was, essentially, my life.

The discipline wasn't just about the schedule. I went three years without touching sugar. My parents threw a birthday party for me every year. There'd be a birthday cake but I wouldn't eat a slice because I'd committed to eating no sugar at all. I was simply not putting that in my body.

Likewise, I didn't drink alcohol at all in college. I didn't take any drugs in college. My focus was the gym, and I wasn't going to do anything that might get in the way of my workout the next day. There was no chance I would have a hangover because that would've affected my next workout.

That high-level discipline, which I'd learned from my parents, meant I would never risk some negative effect on my training. That's how the 135-pound 16-year-old became a 260-pound 26-year-old who could step onto a stage with others to be the guy with the best physique and fully expect to win.

I knew the discipline would pay off.

You might ask, "Why put in all that effort?" That's a good question with a simple answer: Like so many teens, I didn't like the way I looked. I saw another possibility and as I started to see the results, I was hooked. Those results felt pretty amazing. I began liking the way I looked.

Now, this part sounds a little bit egotistical—because it was—but, when I decided to compete, I committed that no one would outwork me. When I went out to compete, I honestly felt no one has trained harder than me." (I fully believed that.) When I did a show, I stepped onto the stage expecting to win because I knew there was no one more committed and no one who had trained harder than me, and that should more than make up for any genetic advantage they may have had. Now that doesn't mean I always won, but I always knew I could. A 100 percent effort was put into my training and preparation for the show, no excuses!

Additionally, baseball, basketball, football, and tennis were team sports. I could have my best day and still lose if the others didn't play well. I could play poorly other days and we'd win because the others played well enough to cover for me. As a young adult, I decided that I needed to control my destiny. I didn't want to depend on others for my success.

If I wanted to gain weight, there was nothing to keep me from gaining weight—except me. If I had a weakness, it was up to me to correct it. No one could tell me what was possible, only my belief and commitment to being better could control my outcome. This was not a phase of my life where balance existed. Prior to a competition, I actually broke up with Janiene so I wouldn't have any distractions. Thank God she is a forgiving person, or I could have lost the best thing in my life.

So, you might ask, "How much did I give up?" Looking back, I don't feel like I had to give up much at all. In the moment, it may have felt like I was giving up some things. You can't train more than a couple hours a day, but for me, you must train for two hours every single day. You also need to get your meals in, supplement those with protein powders, avoid junk food, and do all the other things that bodybuilding requires. But the result became so positive so quickly that it never felt like much of a sacrifice.

Truths My Father Taught Me

Remember when I mentioned generational change being part of an intentional life? Growing up with my dad showed me success isn't just possible, it's to be expected. He's a retired Colonel and at one point, was Group 3, A Team Commander of the Special Forces out of Fort Bragg, North Carolina. Those groups were numbered, depending on what area of the world they'd deploy to when needed, and were divided into three teams, A, B, and C. The teams were hierarchal, the A-Team being the most senior and the most experienced in what we called "unconventional warfare." Not only was he Special Forces, but he led the team.

When dad was stationed at the Army War College in Carlisle, Pennsylvania, they had a sports day where athletes from all of the different military war colleges came to compete. Dad was playing handball then, and of course, won the handball tournament against all of the other branches' best players. So, being raised in that environment, when I started my real estate career, I had every expectation that I would rise to the top. It was what I had lived growing up. It also helped me understand that the example we set for our children will have a profound impact on the trajectory of their lives—for better or worse.

Discipline, hard work, and success were things I grew up seeing regularly, so leading a disciplined life with ambitious goals and an expectation of success comes naturally for me. What I've come to find out is not having these lessons learned at home while you are growing up doesn't mean they aren't available to you. Regardless of where you are in life, change is in your control.

Mom and Dad also knew the value of work. He came to me just before I turned 16. (This is the kind of conversation we had back then.) He walked up to me and said, "You know, you're gonna be working when you're 16."

"Yes, sir."

"I'm not talking about 'at some point' when you're 16 but, when you turn 16, I expect you to have a job."

"Yes, sir."

And then he walked off.

I think that conversation happened about a month before my birthday. So, the next weekend, I put on dressy, church clothes, hopped onto my bicycle, and rode to the Red Lobster restaurant on the edge of the neighborhood. I walked in, you know the style, wearing a white shirt and black pants, and said, "Hi, can I have an application?"

The hostess said, "Yeah, let me get the manager."

Suddenly, I'm thinking, "Oh, I don't want to have to talk to a manager. I just want to get an application." Well, the manager came out and said, very nicely, "Oh, come on in, sit down," and introduced herself. The conversation went great. She said, "Absolutely, that'd be wonderful. How much do you want to work?"

Dad had said, "You work Friday night, Saturday night, and Sunday during the day."

"If you're available to work those times, you can start next weekend."

"Am I allowed to if I'm not 16?"

"Well, how old are you?"

"I'm 15, still a month away from 16, but I have to have a job that day. I mean, so that's why I'm here."

So that's what I worked through the rest of high school. I bought a little Triumph Spitfire convertible with the money I saved. I drove it all through college. It was a great, early life lesson that, if you're willing to work, you can reach your goals.

I got a job teaching defensive driving that took me through college. I was thrilled with my life, working evenings from 6:00 to 10:00 p.m. and all day Saturday. The rest of the time I was training hard, eating six meals a day, lying in the sun, and making $20 per hour—good money for a kid fresh out of school back then.

Now, you need to understand that I was never super-motivated by money. Army officers get paid well, but not like the private sector. We had what we needed, but we weren't living in a mansion. When I finished college, I had the life I wanted. I was incredibly happy. Mom and Dad were not so happy. Unlike me, they were looking toward my future.

Mom and Dad browbeat me into getting a real estate license. I explained to them that I had no interest in selling houses. They said, "Look, why don't you just get a real estate license? You'll probably buy yourself a few houses in your life and, at least, you'll know something about it."

So, I did. I also stretched the three-week class into six months—that's how enthusiastic I was about the idea. I just told them I was taking classes, and they were thrilled to hear that I was doing something.

I passed the exam and got hired on at a KW office. Remember, this is the late 1980s; Silicon Valley was still a new idea and the "business casual" dress code wasn't a thing. Even if all you were doing was picking up your mail, you wore a coat and tie to the office in Austin, Texas. You don't "pop in" without them. Well, I was a 260-pounder with a 56-inch chest and a 33-inch waist, so I had to have a tailor custom-make a couple of sport coats. There was nothing being made back then for guys like me.

So, I walked in and looked around and said to myself, "I'm making 20 bucks an hour and working 24 hours a week, while these people are selling houses and seem to be doing better than me. If they can do it, then I can certainly sell houses and I don't have to sell many houses to replace the money I'm making now. This could be a better gig for me. I could work less and make more money. That was important for me since having free time was more important than money.

That was my initial thinking. You might say I woke up to what a good gig I could have. Once in, I realized I'm way underachieving. I'm capable of way more than this, and if I get serious, get fully committed to real estate, this could be something big for me.

Why did I react like that?

I don't know; maybe because I'm super competitive. I looked around and thought, "Man, these people are successful, making more money than me and driving great cars. I'm not going to let that happen." I think that, whatever environment I've been in, I look around and say, "Okay, I want to be the best at whatever that is."

Real estate wasn't my lifelong ambition, and for me, it wasn't just about making money. But as usual, for me, it became about being the best. Even if I fell short, since results were judged on number of sales and volume, I knew both of mine would be strong. If I were always pushing myself to be better, trying to be my best, even if I fell short, I would still have impressive results. And I certainly wouldn't be mediocre, just kind of middle of the pack.

No matter what I did, I always wanted to be the best I could. There's no reason you can't be as well. Up for the challenge? Then, let's get to it!

CHAPTER 2

My Mission led to a Vision

My Mission to Change Perception

Myth: High-level success requires sacrificing the unimaginable life everyone dreams of living

I mentioned that I've frequently met people who are extremely wealthy but extremely unhappy. They've sacrificed the unimaginable life for what they define as success. They perceived success in one way but, in many cases, it turned out that the success they dreamed of wasn't as great as they thought it would be.

That's not to say there are no sacrifices to be made. No one has a perfect life; we all have to make sacrifices. We make them willingly because we believe the end result will be worth more to us than what we gave up getting that result.

There are things worth sacrificing for. We all know that. But to sacrifice everything just for money or a job title or what you perceive to be success rarely works out the way you expected. The excuse that you can't be there for your family because you're trying to create something that will benefit them in the end is just that, an excuse, and eventually you'll see the damage that excuse created. Personal and family happiness—all the joy that you can experience in life along the way—to give that up for any other success is completely unnecessary.

When my wife, Janiene, and I were in our 20s, we became close friends of another young couple. The wife had a twin sister living in Florida who was married to the remarkably successful owner of multiple new car dealerships. They were invited to visit Florida, and they asked us to join them.

I'm telling you, when we pulled up and saw this massive stucco wall around this compound, my jaw dropped. The back of the compound was the ocean and there were multiple boat docks with boats down by the water. The main house was massive. I don't know how big, but the guest house we stayed in was 5,000 square feet and the other guest house was about 3,500 square feet. All that plus tennis courts, pools–you name it, they seemed to have it.

Our friend's brother-in-law and I made an instant connection. Like me, he got up early every day to work out. Our visit lasted four days, and each day, we went to the gym together. On the way home, we went to the same diner where he ate the same breakfast–egg whites and chicken breast. Same waitress, same meal, same diner, every day. As we sat across the table from each other, we talked.

He was considerably older than me and told me about what he called his "first round" in life. He had a wife and kids but everything about his world centered on business–making more money, expanding his business, buying more dealerships, generating even more money–growth, growth, growth.

As a result, his relationship with his wife failed and he never really connected with his children. Basically, they grew up without him because he was always focused on work. As you'd guess, it all came crashing down around him. When he recovered from that, he decided to start again, and learn from his mistakes.

He remarried–I think she was at least 20 years younger than him–and, with her, he did what he called his "do-over." He started his personal life again, very differently. He reinvented himself.

What interested me most was his new priorities. He started working just a few hours a day, in the middle of the day, from home. He was the one who took the kids he had with his new wife to school and picked them up from school because he wanted to be present. Every morning, he got up and went to the gym because his health hadn't been a priority in the first round. Going to the gym early every morning, where it doesn't take time away from the kids, was a part of that plan.

That's how we came to sit at his diner, with him eating his high-protein breakfast. As we ate, I was fascinated, listening as he explained the mistakes he'd made with his first life and how he was determined not to repeat those mistakes.

This was a great lesson to see firsthand. As my business grew and I became more successful and entered into the mastermind group, Gary Keller reinforced what I learned from that man. Gary said it's all about "God, family, business," and that came from the guy who owned the business. Everything he taught us could be summed up by saying "Yes, we make sacrifices, but we're not here to sacrifice so we can do more business. We're here to do more business so we can have a better life."

Those were the two moments that set me on the course to write this book:

- An introduction to someone who had failed miserably but changed course and became successful at what truly matters.
- Instruction from my own business leader that stressed other priorities over business. From the beginning, he taught us, we didn't want to run our lives the way so many others had. (It all went back to the calendar and all that went on the calendar.)

Now fast forward in my career to where I'm working with many successful people. I'm certainly not saying that all wealthy people are miserable. I don't mean to paint with such a broad brush. I would say it's shocking how many of the wealthy people I've worked with have been unhappy people. We've all heard that money doesn't buy happiness, but I have gotten to live it through some of my clients.

My Vision: Exceptional Results

In contrast to that car dealer in Florida, I had Dad. He retired after 24 or 25 years in the military, and my parents started buying small rental houses. This was back in the early 1980s, and my folks wound up with fifty rent houses, all of them owned free and clear.

I should point out that both started out life with basically nothing. I could show you the houses they grew up in, and you'd be shocked. Dad's house in San Antonio didn't have air conditioning, so in many nights, he slept with his head by a window, or even out on the front porch, in hopes of catching a breeze. San Antonio is extremely hot—100 degrees— and very humid—40 percent-plus. They didn't grow up with much. So as adults, they worked hard, managed all the properties themselves, and created amazing positive cash flow from those properties. Mom would frequently say that the most important thing they could do with their money was buy time with our family.

Maybe that doesn't sound all that exceptional. In practical terms, it wasn't; it was what millions of families did in previous generations. But, in terms of what we see today, with all the problems families have, I call it exceptional, and I count myself exceptionally lucky to have grown up in a family where time together was a priority.

Be Disciplined

Discipline is trading what you want now for what you want most.

I discussed this in detail in the introduction, so I'll just say this: I believe discipline is something that is completely within your control and is inside all of us. When I was growing up, I was frequently called lazy. Because of how my parents had to grow up working from as early as they remember, they didn't understand how I wouldn't naturally gravitate to doing more, getting up earlier, being more productive, etc. For me, I wasn't disciplined to go conquer the world each day when I was young, because I hadn't discovered the things that really motivated me. Years later, when my parents called me to say they had read that I was ranked number 15 in the nation in *The Wall Street Journal*, my mom laughingly asked, "How can you be number 15 at anything?" remembering the kid who loved to sleep in on weekends and do as little as he could get away with. It was much easier for me to be disciplined when I found something that really motivated me. So to those parents for whom this sounds only too familiar, just know, the road is long enough for all kids to find their motivation—even yours!

Figure out what works for you and stick to it. You can be successful if you're not disciplined but, without discipline, I bet that you'll never achieve your unimaginable life and you'll work a whole lot harder while not doing it.

Be Confident

I don't remember ever even thinking about a career when I was in high school. Though some have a clear vision for their future early in their lives, I was slower to get to that point. In fact, I don't know that I ever gave my career a single serious thought.

I'm a confident person. So I knew that, whatever I finally landed on, I would be fine. I never felt like I was going to struggle. During college, my focus was the gym and all I really cared about was my ability to train and compete. I didn't care about how I dressed or what I drove. I cared about my training. I felt like, "Man, look at what I've created!" I was immensely proud of the 135-pound kid who'd become a 260-pound man who could legitimately compete with other bodybuilders.

My successes in sports and bodybuilding gave me a deep sense of pride and confidence. My life was never about making money, but because I'm so competitive, the money naturally came with success. For me, it was being competitive and succeeding at what I did.

Before real estate, I loved my life. I loved the idea that I got to lay in the sun every day. I got to train for two hours. I got to eat my six meals a day and hang out at home. That doesn't sound like a guy who's driven to be successful. I know I'm not. I'm the guy who's driven to be happy and I'm confident that, whatever I do, I'll be successful, and more importantly, I'll be happy.

Be Intentional

At the end of my first full year in real estate, two guys came to me and proposed a partnership. This was the first team approach that I'd ever heard of in real estate. Their plan was simple: we all work and throw the money into a pot and split the pot three ways at the end of each month. Now, I should tell you, I quit working the last two months of the previous year because I hit my goal early on, so I just took the time off. (I could do that partly because of business I got through Motorola, which was relocating a lot of their employees to Austin at that time.)

One of my prospective partners did three times my business the previous year and the other guy did five times mine. I went home to Janiene and I said, "Sweetie, you know, I got these two guys who want me to join. They've both been in real estate for years. One of the guys had been the top producer in the city. So I'm thinking, I got to come home and talk to you about this because you know me. I'm competitive. If I'm going to be a part of this group, I'm not going to be number three in the group. In a pretty short time, I'm going to be number one because it's just that important to me.

"I need to know if you're okay with that. I'm going to have to work much harder. I'll have to change the way I do things. I'd be working a whole lot more. Are you okay with that?" (Remember, we're still in our twenties.)

She said (although she probably doesn't even remember the conversation), "Sweetie, I've been waiting for you to grow up. I'm great with that."

She was dead serious. She said it in a kind, loving way, not in an angry way, but serious!

And, I thought, "Well, there you go." Ultimately, the partnership lasted about nine years. By year three, I was the top producer and remained so for the rest of my time with them.

Motivations vary. I am incredibly competitive, and in that partnership, I intended to be the top producer. It was a conscious decision, but let me be clear on this—not mine alone. I proposed it and it was seconded by my wife, my partner in all other areas of my life. Because of that, she supported me 100 percent in what it took to make that goal happen.

Maybe success happens by accident, sometimes. Even if it does, the best successes always happen because of a well-considered, carefully reviewed decisions that everyone involved signs on to.

Be Exceptional

You've probably heard of people, super-successful salespeople, who started selling at 15 or 16, bought his or her first company at 19 or 20, and just went up from there. That wasn't me. They were driven from a young age. My story's completely different.

I mentioned that after college, I was still teaching defensive driving. That allowed me to hang out and train as much as I liked, so I was perfectly content. I was living what, for me, at that moment, was "my best life." Mom and Dad were not so content. They "suggested" I get my real estate license. As I mentioned, my folks' impression of me in high school and through college, looking back, was that I was a pretty typical lazy kid. Well, it took me six months to finish a three-week course, so yeah, they probably had something there.

In contrast, one of my partners would brag that he'd worked sixty or seventy days in a row without a day off. I looked at him and it became very clear, very quickly, that he was probably working at 60 percent efficiency. It became equally clear that he wasn't happy. He'd just come into the office, well, drag himself in might better describe it. He didn't want to make calls and didn't do this and didn't do that—just moped around—but he'd never take time off.

This was prior to my work with Gary Keller, but it was really interesting to see and very obvious. I could see the way he worked and instantly knew, though I was years from fully understanding the whole 80 percent and Life Pie ideas, that his way wasn't the right way. Even so, I saw others doing the same thing. Maybe at different levels, but similar behavior.

Maybe you've heard a story like this: a salesman comes home from the annual meeting and tells his wife that the "big prize" for the top sales rep in the company would be an all-expense-paid trip to Hawaii or some other spectacular place. His wife responds, "I don't want to see you in this house until 9:30 p.m. any night for the next year!"

She wants that trip, and that's fair, I would, too (especially after our family trips to Hawaii!). But is that the way to get there? Too many salespeople think it's all about numbers: make this many phone calls or contacts, schedule this many presentations, close this percentage of them, and there you are! That used to be the standard model of sales success. It worked, but it had a price.

That partner of mine thought like that. As a result, everything else behind him was a mess. His family relationship, well, let's just say, it wasn't great. He got home in the summer after having an appointment that took until nine o'clock and his wife would be livid. "Like every other night, you are always working." (Whether she said exactly that or not, the attitude came through loud and clear.)

By contrast, if I got home at nine o'clock at night, Janiene would have a meal waiting for me in the warming drawer and say, "Sweetie, I'm so sorry you had such a long day. Come on, sit down and eat." Her attitude, as much as anything else, was a key to my success. I made working long days the exception to the rule, so I didn't burn out, and she encouraged me when I got in late, instead of making me feel that working long days somehow slighted our time together. Both contributed to my measure of success.

By contrast, knowing that you'll be in trouble for working late takes away a positive feeling that should be coming from the other areas of your life when you're having to put in the extra hours at work. As a result, working every day, without a break, may have been a way to stay away from the challenging environment at home. Bad decisions compound each other, resulting in neither of them getting what they want—a happier marriage.

Today, we should know better. "Quality not quantity" or "work smarter, not harder," are the modern mantras for many salespeople, but not all. Consciously, intentionally balancing family and work and other aspects is still, I think, the exception, rather than the rule. By having a clear plan, you can be that exception.

Unimaginable Life

For me, the life that I live now and have lived for the last almost 30 years was unimaginable when I was a kid and young adult because I didn't think I could live such a life. I didn't have to imagine this life; I saw it as a young man, and I believed you had to be a superstar athlete or major movie star or something like that to have it.

When I was growing up, those were the people who lived this kind of life and I honestly didn't know that anyone else could. So, it was unimaginable that I could put myself in that position. Yes, I imagined a life that's all of these things, but I never imagined myself having them because I wasn't the Super Bowl champ or the action hero. That life was for this very select few. Today, however, I'm blessed to have gotten to live this life. That doesn't mean I make billions or have ten mansions and a private jet, but my family and I have not only everything we need but, within reason, anything we want.

The "unimaginable life" will mean different things to different people based on many factors. As I mentioned earlier, I didn't start out with a life solely based on money and I still don't; I have other priorities.

I'm still a competitive person. I still want to be the best all the time. Certainly, the best that I can be and, whenever possible, the best performer in whatever group I'm in. I use other people as motivation. I think what I fear more than anything else is mediocrity. I would rather fail miserably than feel like I have settled. The opportunity to succeed at a high level far outweighs any fear of failing.

In coming up with my definition of the unimaginable life, I was thinking in purely practical terms—my day-to-day existence. Today, I get to live the very day-to-day life that I never figured I could.

So, I've mentioned the Life Pie and 80 percent a couple of times now. What specifically do I mean?

That will differ for each of us. My Pie is divided into five segments because those are my priorities. I know of people who divide their Life Pies into six or ten or twelve segments. If it works for them, I'm all for it but I feel like five is a manageable number because you don't divide your attention too many ways. Here are my five Life Pie slices as an example to help you decide on yours: The risk in giving you five pieces of my Life Pie is that you will copy them as your own, and the point of this is to list the top five areas of **your** life where you would like to see improvement and create goals and then action items to achieve them. Later, I'll mention several other areas you can consider as options for your Life Pie.

Personal

This Personal category is for anything **you** want to accomplish. In other words, look a year into the future and decide what would make you feel like this was a great year for you personally. If you have a passion for playing the drums and dream of performing in a band on stage someday and put that dream in the Personal section of your Life Pie; it means this is the year for you to act! Buy a drum set, take lessons, and eventually, join a band. If you've always wanted to climb a mountain somewhere far away, put it on your Life Pie, move it to your goals, create an action plan, and this is the year you'll make it happen. It's really amazing; put your dreams on paper, create a timeline, and make them happen. This is the life you choose, not the one you were dealt. It may be challenging for some of you to believe this works but as someone who has lived his adult life this way, it's real.

Two years ago, as I write this, I competed in a bodybuilding contest after 32 years off the stage. Why? Because after years of thinking about it, it was finally important enough to make it to my Life Pie. I needed to know if I could still compete so many years later. Because I credit so much in my life to my time in the gym, I've always trained. I've always loved the gym; it was, for a long time, my greatest passion. So I'm always making time to workout. As I've gotten older, certain limitations have crept in because, well, they just do as we age. I'm having to eat a little more carefully, typically avoid things that don't contribute to my well-being, and certainly train differently in the gym.

The training, by the way, for that show was brutal. My expectation was that I would revert back to my **much** younger self, and things would just fall in place. You might think this falls under the category: "Be careful what you wish for," but I have no regrets. It was a goal of mine, and the time was finally right for me to reach that goal. It was also an opportunity for my adult kids to see me compete. When we had our first, competing took a back seat to being a dad…and adulting!

The personal slice is all about being intentional about fulfilling your internal wants or needs.

Spiritual

Remember, this is an example of **my** Life Pie. If it helps you, follow whatever part of my example fits you. If not, use it as an example and choose a piece that better fits your life.

I believe spirituality is a good thing for people and for society. My relationship with God is particularly important. I'm not here to preach or convert but to share my experience. For me, a large part of that experience is giving back.

All my life, I have heard, "It's better to give than to receive" but, until you actually start giving, you can't imagine how it makes you feel. I've been so blessed with the life I have that it's enabled me to carve out a little bit of money to help others. For example:

As I write this, I look back two years to a man I saw on a corner the day before Thanksgiving. I had seen him there for the last couple of years, smiling and waving to everyone driving by. Because years earlier, I'd read an article written by the sister of a homeless man who said that every time we give them money, we are prolonging their time on the streets, keeping them away from the help they could receive from their families or their community. I no longer give money directly to homeless people, but, being the day before Thanksgiving, I get a $20 bill out of my pocket. As he comes over, I see he's about my age, a bald African-American man using a walker. I said clearly, "Hey, this is for a Thanksgiving meal tomorrow, okay? You've got to promise me no drinks, no cigarettes, not anything else. This is for food."

He said, "No, I don't do any of that."

He excitedly showed me his ID card, and I saw that the next day, Thanksgiving, was his birthday. Not really taking notice of that, I gave him $20 and went on about my business.

The next morning, I woke up to Thanksgiving and lots of things for me to get done. We were expecting twenty-plus family members at the house, but I was feeling convicted. Janiene noticed it.

She asked, "What's the matter?" She can always tell when something's off. She's right. All these people are coming over and I'm thinking about Vincent, the guy from the corner, and how sad it must be for him to go have his birthday meal alone. So, I told her about the money I gave him. She then encouraged me. "You need to go then and see if he's up there, and if he is, go have breakfast with him."

So, as I headed over there, I'm praying that he'd be back at his corner. Thankfully, he was there, and not only did we have breakfast, but I got eight of the servers to come over and sing happy birthday to him when they brought his piece of chocolate cake with a candle in the middle of it. That started a friendship that continues today. The following Thanksgiving, he was at our house, among the twenty-something family members. Because he's very spiritual, he goes to church with us on Sunday mornings, and we then go out to eat at the same place we had his birthday meal, and just hang out—me, Janiene, and Vincent—most Sundays.

We decided he needed more than just a Thanksgiving meal and Sunday mornings together. So, we pay part of the rent for the two-bedroom apartment he shares with another person near where I met him. We've helped him fill out the paperwork to get him on the list for this really cool charity called Community First that gives tiny homes to homeless people. I think Vincent will be my friend for the rest of my life. He's a great human being.

Had giving not made it to the spiritual section of my Life Pie, I wouldn't have been open to that initial meeting, and our friendship wouldn't have been possible.

I've come to believe that, if you're open to it, there are really amazing things that can happen to you in life. Likewise, if you're so focused on money that every dollar matters to you, giving $20 away to a total stranger who's not working, you might think, "Well, he should be working, that's on him." You know, that's a whole weirdly negative mindset. If you don't let money alone control your actions, really cool things can happen in life. When you're so blessed that you have enough money to help other people, it's an amazing feeling to watch the changes that can happen.

I want to leave this life feeling that God was able to do a little of His work through me, making good things happen to others. And I don't want to wait around for Him to provide me with opportunities. Again, being intentional means wonderful things (maybe big things, but mostly, I think, they will be small things) are going to happen because I was looking for those opportunities.

The spiritual slice is about building and maintaining a relationship that works with God. For me, it's a big part of my Life Pie.

Family

We all have families, and mine is a driving force in my life, which is why this category is a piece of my Life Pie. Likely, I learned it from my parents that time with family is a top priority. You're not going to have as great a relationship as you can have with your child if you're not intentional. When we had our first child, I was excited to be involved in everything I could, and coach every sport our son was involved in. When our daughter came along, I made the same goal. I wanted to be there, all the time, with something that was important to them so they could see that what was important to them was also important to me. And most of all, I wanted them to know they were my priority. I wanted to be involved and celebrate their successes and help them learn from their failures.

Being involved that way was critical to me and that became a priority on my calendar. Other things were scheduled around their practices, games, and tournaments.

Family vacations also became a priority. As the kids grew older, time with extended family was a big part of our family vacations. As a result, our extended family has always been remarkably close, and my kids have amazing relationships with my parents and their cousins.

The family slice is also a beautiful place for being intentional about your relationship with your spouse or significant other. Being intentional about your relationship with the most important person in your life may seem obvious but, as is the case with most things, doing nothing and expecting a great outcome is a strategy for failure. If you're having issues at home, can you imagine the difference it would make if you said "I love you" many times throughout the day—when you wake up, when you leave the house, when you go to bed at night, on every phone call, etc. Or, what if you brought flowers home every month, just because, or you were the driving force behind regular date nights together.

Remember, look a year into the future and ask what would make it feel like it was a momentous year with your spouse, then do the very small things it would take for that to happen.

The family slice is about building and improving relationships with my parents, my spouse, my children, and my extended family.

Financial

The amazing thing about this piece of pie is the earlier you start implementing a financial plan, the unbelievable difference it makes in the outcome. And putting in your Life Pie to teach your kids about finances at an early age will give them a huge advantage for the rest of their lives.

I'm not being redundant; work is work and money is money. They are related but far from identical. For example, part of the financial slice may include paying for kids' college and weddings, having the money to retire comfortably, leaving a legacy, being in a position to help others when needed, and so on.

Some of the items in your personal piece or family piece may require financial support, so there needs to be a place for you to prioritize, and create a plan for the money needed. Or, if like my parents, you've always dreamed of having rental property that gives you cash flow, you need to plan to get the money to purchase your first property. By being intentional and putting it on your Life Pie, you will actually take the step to create the plan to save that money and create a timeline that will get you to your first purchase.

The reason that I started *The 80 Percent Project* was because, for years, I've seen the need firsthand and knew I could have influence. I knew for years that this was something I would eventually do, but finally putting it on my Life Pie meant it was finally time. Creating a successful business certainly falls into the financial piece of your Life Pie. That business can also be part of your legacy which can also be part of this financial slice.

The financial slice comprises every aspect of your financial well-being and the recognition that all aspects of your financial well-being are interrelated.

Professional (Work)

At the end of the day, unless you are independently wealthy, you have to make money. I have to support myself and my family, so work has to be there. However, I created *The 80 Percent Project* to help you work to live, not live to work. Since this is the daily work you do, look a year into the future and decide what it would take for this to have been a wonderful year at work. If you work for someone, it may be a promotion, or a raise this year. If those things are important to you, they are important enough for you to create a plan to make them happen. Remember, being intentional makes the goals become reality.

This is exceptionally important for me while I'm running *The 80 Percent Project* and my real estate sales business at the same time. My work piece includes individual goals for each business, along with the action items required to hit those goals.

For most of us, this is the part of our life that tends to dominate our time and attention. There isn't necessarily anything wrong with that, as long as you use the other pieces of your pie to provide balance. Though I've intentionally put this piece last, most will consider it to be the most important part of their lives, which is exactly why the Life Pie becomes critical to your happiness. The fact that for many people, work occupies most of their waking hours doesn't mean it's more important than your other pieces. It just may require more of your time.

The following chapters will provide tools to assist you in working more effectively so you can free up more of your time and attention for the other Life Pie slices.

Generational Change

Children are a Product of What They Live

People look at the phrase "generational change" and the first thing they usually think of is money. "I'm going to make a generational change because I didn't get anything from my parents, but my kids are going to get something from me."

This certainly is generational change, but there's something so much bigger than that—the example you're setting for them. Your children should go out into the world with the sure knowledge that they can accomplish whatever they want to accomplish. If they've heard it, they may, but their chances for success are so much greater if they've seen their parents do it and lived it their whole lives. Moreover, if they've lived it their whole lives feeling that they were still the priority, that lesson will be passed down for generations to come.

Both of my children are incredibly confident because I felt that confidence was the best thing I could teach them. Because I was intentional about being involved when they were growing up, I was intentional about demonstrating that they were always a high priority in my life. Even when I was putting up the highest numbers—having nationally recognized success with Keller-Williams—I made it clear that I wouldn't sacrifice my family time to achieve it.

I think a lot of successful people still believe that sacrificing their family time will create generational change. They're right, but it isn't the change they expect or want. By sacrificing the time that their children need with them when they're still young, they lose their connection to those kids. Instead of learning how to be successful, they learn about money.

That can go two ways:

- They may learn, from your example, that money is the all-consuming priority. They become greedy, social-climbers or corporate types for whom winning is everything and will likely pass this attitude on to their kids.
- They may reject money as a priority. If they do, they may be happier, initially, but they also may not give career preparation the priority it needs. So they'll get stuck in low-paying, mediocre jobs that don't provide for themselves and their family properly. Because they didn't get the attention they needed when they were young, they may overcorrect as adults and never realize a level of success they were capable of attaining.

There's another possibility. If you're successful enough to provide a living for them, you may destroy them. I was shocked by a story I heard of a lawyer whose whole practice was retirement planning. He dealt with a lot of very wealthy men and women who set up a trust fund for each child. They'd never have to work a day in their lives. That lawyer said that many of those "trust fund babies" never accomplished anything of value for themselves or others. They didn't feel a need to learn anything, and in many cases, they didn't care about anything, except themselves. They lacked initiative, and though they had a tremendous opportunity to give to the world, charity or community service never crossed their minds. If my kids had turned out like that, I would feel like I robbed them of ever knowing what they were capable of accomplishing, and that would be tough to live with.

True, I'm going to leave them money, but my children are already old enough to be out on their own and both are doing well. They've learned the value of initiative and they have a plan for their lives. That's a clear generational change from their dad, the guy who initially lived for the gym, the sun, and a job that earned me just enough to get by.

It's the habits, the beliefs, which make generational change. Let's look at some history:

Baby boomers (now passing 60) and Gen Xers (40s and 50s) grew up without technology. We had to look people in the face in meetings. Many of us learned practical skills in shop and home economics classes. We averaged over forty hours of work per week. Gen Yers or Millennials (late 20s to early 40s) average less than forty hours. Many lack basic skills like literacy, math, and problem-solving. They text and work remotely instead of in an office.

Many younger people were "latch-key kids" from families where both parents worked, brought home fast food as often as they cooked dinner, and were too tired to spend the time their children needed from them. It's no wonder marriage numbers are down, families are smaller, and divorce runs rampant. It's not hard to see why Gen X and Gen Y are experiencing severe health problems (like cancer) earlier in life and even more frequently than Boomers.

Every generation inherits problems from their parents and grandparents. Today, the world needs to recognize that sad fact and turn it around. Look at what our parents did right and do more of it, and learn what they did wrong and fix it. The family is the best place to make those changes. As I said before, it's never too late to change—the way we do things and what we teach our children. Even if those children are in their 30s and 40s, it's not too late to learn. Rethink and reset your priorities to include financial and familial success. Help your children teach your grandchildren. That will create generational change.

Teach Your Children by Example

Family comes first, even while creating exceptional business results.

- I always treated their mother with love and respect.
- I showed them they were a priority when they were young by always being involved.
- We (my wife and I) spent time with them on vacations, some with extended family.
- We encouraged them to work early in life, creating a good habit for adulthood.
- I visited their grandparents regularly.

Passing Down Lessons for Generations to Come

The classic "American Dream" is usually described as me having more than my parents did and passing on more to my children than I had. That's a solid, positive view of the economic American dream—I make more money; I have two cars instead of one; I have a more generous retirement plan. It's great, and parents should teach their children the work ethic that'll make that dream possible.

Let's add some innovative ideas to that dream:

I wanted my kids to go out into the world better prepared to deal with the world than I was. They know how to be successful at work and in life because I taught them everything I know. They'll start farther along the path than I did and, maybe, do far more than I did. We gave them opportunities to fail and to succeed and to fail and succeed again and to learn from it so that, at some point, they would look up and say, "Look what I created."

I wanted my children to have strong families. I think we did everything we could to show the kids that we love them more than any business success—that they were always our highest priority. They seem to have become well-adjusted adults who are ready to face what's out there in the world.

One other thing:

So many people say, "That's just the way I am, I can't change." Well, why did all those Europeans come to America? For freedom—freedom to earn more, to worship the way they wanted—to have a better life. Did that stop with the Pilgrims? Why did Daniel Boone settle in Kentucky? Why did a half million 49ers go to California? Why do Americans still attend tent revival meetings? Change is part of America; it's in our DNA. It isn't easy, never has been, but I've changed over time, so have you. It's natural as we grow up and, mostly, we don't even think about it; it just happens. So how about we take control of that change? How about part of that American Dream is realizing that, regardless of our age or situation, we need change, we can change, and there are people who can help us change. My kids can be better people in every respect than I was, and I can be a better person than I used to be. That, too, would be a fitting example to our children and grandchildren.

"Family" is More than Family

The most important generational change will be within your immediate family. Does it end there?

It can, but it shouldn't. You have other "families"—your work family, your church family, your neighborhood family—whatever group you're a part of, has similarities to a family. Think about the younger people specifically, but really, everybody in those groups. You have an opportunity to start other generational changes by mentoring co-workers, congregation members, and neighbors.

As a business owner or manager, you need to provide training so your people can do their jobs right. Well, are job skills the only things you can teach your people? If you want them to advance, to be more valuable to the company, you should also teach supervisory skills and skills outside their specific job. Maybe they'll help grow your company with you. Maybe they'll take what you taught them and find a better job at a higher pay rate than you could offer them. If they do, take it as a compliment.

It doesn't have to be something big. Minor changes can, over time, become very big influences in other people's lives. Who knows what the little help we've given to Vincent will grow into in ten or twenty years.

Don't limit yourself. Wherever you can create a positive change, do it!

CHAPTER 3

The Life Pie

Life can be rough. Maybe work goes slow; you and your spouse might have a serious disagreement; a sudden bill arises, putting your finances into a tailspin. Some days you really should've just stayed in bed.

On those days when some aspect of your life is exploding in your face, you need a cushion to land on. In my life, I've defined my top five priorities—family, financial, personal, professional, and spiritual. Each is closely related to the others (and my goals for each may overlap) but I keep them as separate as possible so that, when my professional efforts get overwhelming, the other four priorities in my life help me relax. When finances have been tight, I could sit back and say, "God, I know you'll help me get through this," and I can rely on my family to do their part.

Think of it as sitting on a stool. If it has three legs, it's perfectly stable but, if one leg breaks, you fall over. If it has five or six legs, chances are it'll wobble a little, but one can break without spilling you into an embarrassing heap on the floor.

LIFE PIE

Have Goals for Each Area of Your Life Pie

I can't count all the books now available about setting and achieving goals. Many of them are worth reading, so, I'm not going to try and outdo them here, but I will summarize. An effective goal is:

1. Quantifiable

It has to be specific, measurable, and scheduled. A financial goal might be, "We will add $18,000 to our savings by December 31st this year." That is unmistakably clear. You can also break it down into short-term steps. If I want an additional $18,000 in savings at the end of the year, I must, on average, add $1,500 per month or $375 per week.

Most people use a monthly budget because we have set costs—taxes, mortgages, car payments, utilities, and other regular expenses that we pay monthly. That leads to an obvious question: "Can I take $1,500 out of the money left after those payments without causing hardship?" If not, do I reduce the savings contribution or do I cut other things like entertainment, contributions to charities, or do I look for additional income sources?

You might consider: Did I get (or will I get) a year-end bonus from work? Can I depend on that to be part of the savings plan? Do I have an investment portfolio with interest and dividends coming in? What sources of income have I outside of regular employment? All these things will figure into your savings plan of action.

In the final analysis, if you can't quantify your goal, you'll never know if you succeeded or failed.

2. Challenging & Inspiring

Why?

It's the most important question to ask when developing a goal. Why this thing, this amount, this timetable? What benefit will I get from achieving this goal as outlined?

If you can't answer that question, you're not developing a goal that motivates you to action.

Habit #2: Begin With the End in Mind is based on imagination—the ability to envision in your mind what you cannot, at present, see with your eyes. It is based on the principle that all things are created twice. There is a mental (first) creation, and a physical (second) creation. The physical creation follows the mental, just as a building follows a blueprint.

If you don't make a conscious effort to visualize who you are and what you want in life, then you empower other people and circumstances to shape you and your life by default.

–Stephen R. Covey[1]

By the way, this is a direct outgrowth of Covey's "Habit #1: Be Proactive," which is what you're doing when you quantify a goal. Once you decide to do something, you need to understand clearly in your own mind, the point of the effort. How will your life change if you accomplish this goal? What positives will follow that success? How will your life change if you fail to accomplish this goal? What negatives will follow that failure? What effort does this require, what costs must you pay, how much time will you spend?

How will you feel if you achieve it? If you don't achieve it? If you don't even try?

As I mentioned earlier, after decades off the stage, I entered a bodybuilding competition in my late 50s. Training was brutal, and I didn't look anything like I thought I would, so was it a waste of time and effort? No, I felt the need to test myself—against myself more than against those guys. I proved one thing to myself, that I still had the discipline to compete. Also, I proved that I had the self-awareness to know that I would've regretted not trying. I tried and I have no regrets.

The Chinese say, "The journey of a thousand miles begins with a single step."

What lies at the end of that road that is so important that you'll go a thousand miles to see it?

---

[1] Stephen R. Covey, "Habit 2: Begin With the End in Mind," The Seven Habits of Highly Successful People. New York City: Free Press (an imprint of Simon & Schuster), 1989. Reprinted at https://www.franklincovey.com/the-7-habits/habit-2/, accessed 22 June 2024.

3. Realistic

As a 135-pound teenager, I read the Charles Atlas ads in the back of my comic books and I decided that's what I wanted to look like. Was that realistic or a fantasy? At the time, those thoughts never occurred to me. Charles Atlas had done it, or so the ads implied, so I could do it. It took years but, during that time, gradual changes took place that I could see, and those changes encouraged me to continue on to my "Charles Atlas" weight of about 260 pounds.

As a competing bodybuilder, I couldn't set winning as a realistic goal. The judges chose the winner and "the best" is a qualitative judgment, not a quantitative judgment.

What's the difference?

- "This thing is 12 inches long," is a **quantitative** judgment; it's measurable by anyone and they'll all get the same answer.
- "This thing is long enough," is a **qualitative** judgment; the end use (an outside factor) tells me if it's true or not.

Each judge picked "the best" based on his individual opinion of what the perfect physique looks like and how close each competitor got to that standard. It would've been totally unrealistic for me to say, "I need to win X number of competitions to be successful." I didn't decide who won. In bodybuilding as in life, we can rarely control the end result, but we can have complete control over our effort.

I could control how I trained. I studied to learn the best techniques for a championship physique and I applied those techniques consistently. I ate a high-protein diet, I avoided sugar and alcohol, and I lifted weights for hours every single day. I focused on the things I was taught would get me looking the way I wanted to look.

I call my current lifestyle the unimaginable life because, as a child, I only saw championship-winning athletes and box-office superstars living that life. I didn't have the skills or drive to play in the major leagues, and I couldn't sing or dance or act well enough that a producer would pay me $10 million. At that time, living this life would've been an unrealistic goal. I couldn't see a path to success. As an adult, I found that path through real estate and my desire to live this life became a realistic goal.

Realistic goals have a clear (if difficult) path to success.

4. Appropriate to Your Values

Returning to a financial goal, people invest in stocks hoping that the price will go up so they can sell at a big profit while earning dividends along the way. It's an obvious path to success.

Would you buy stock in a distillery? The market is secure—we proved that in the 1920s when Prohibition failed—people are going to drink. The return on investment can be extremely high—people pay big bucks for premium booze. Suppose, however, you're a teetotaler—is that how you want to fund your retirement? The same is true of an anti-gambling family and casinos, or anti-smoking families and tobacco companies. If you have strong political opinions, you probably won't invest in companies that support opposing views. If you're an environmentalist, you probably won't invest in companies that you feel are polluters. If you're a pacifist, you probably won't invest in companies with strong military ties.

There are a lot of people who share the mindset of *The Godfather* movies, "It's not personal, it's just business."[2] They make money however they can and they don't lose sleep over what other people do. For some, it would be a little hypocritical to profit from what you call a vice or to support things for money that you wouldn't support in other areas of life. Just remember, as you go through this process of change, you are creating your own perfect life, so what you include in your journey is completely up to you.

"Synergy" means all the pieces work together to accomplish more than any piece could accomplish on its own. The Life Pie only works because each slice supports the others.

My suggestion is that you set goals that you wouldn't be ashamed to make public—to your family and friends, your pastor, or your God.

---

[2] *The Godfather*, screenplay by Mario Puzo & Francis Ford Coppola, based on the novel by Mario Puzo; directed by Francis Ford Coppola. Paramount Pictures Corp., 1972.

Create Ten-, Five-, Three-, and One-year Goals

Do a Missing Person Report on Yourself

What do you want your life to look like 10 years down the road? Let's jump ahead, mentally. Your future self is missing and you're filing a missing person report with the police. What does he or she look like?

- I'm wearing these clothes.
- I drive this car.
- I live in this area.
- I spend my time doing this and that.
- Here's the best place to find me.

That's a funny analogy but it's better than what one fellow used to ask his employees: "What do you want on your tombstone?"

Let me give you a couple of examples of my goals to show you how you might organize yours. Notice that I mix my family and work goals because those two affect each other significantly:

Goals/Slice	Family/Work	Personal
Ten Years	1. We'll go on one annual trip (that we pay for) with the kids and grandkids. 2. We'll still live in the same house. 3. Move Dad (then aged 100) to Austin.	1. To spend a lot of time traveling with Janiene. 2. To spend a lot of time being grandparents.
Five Years	1. To have my team handle all real estate. 2. To begin the process of selling the coaching business.	1. Start a restaurant chain situated near college campuses.
Three Years	1. Do 50% more real estate business than today—all in the luxury arena. 2. Have my daughter running a coaching business with fifteen-plus coaches working for us.	1. Compete in one final bodybuilding contest. 2. Start shopping for a vacation home in Colorado. 3. Convince both children to move back to Austin.

Goals/Slice	Family/Work	Personal
One Year	1. A family vacation in Hawaii over Thanksgiving, Vail with Janiene. 2. Expand luxury marketing campaign. 3. Book release, schedule years of speaking engagements.	1. Keep my body weight at 220, so I can present my best self on stage. 2. Have breakfast with Dad every week. Call him at least once per day.

Now, you might think my personal five-year goal is really a work goal. It is, totally, but you see how my personal and work goals are intertwined. In five years, I expect to be "retired" from the businesses that I've built. I think I want to do something different, something fun—for me, my employees, and my customers. That goal isn't about money; it's about having fun in retirement.

One-Year Goals are an Action Plan to be Adjusted Along the Way

If you're always paying attention to your goals, then you're always adjusting.

For example, the National Association of Realtors reported that 49 percent of Realtors sold no houses or one house in 2023—that's half of all licensed Realtors. My dues are a couple of thousand dollars per year plus continuing education costs and the costs of operating my office. Now, we all know there are a lot of Realtors who work part-time or don't do much with it, but these are licensed Realtors who are still paying to be Realtors. I think that speaks volumes. They are not doing what it takes to be successful. Some are new and learning, others just "dabble" and aren't trying to make their living entirely in real estate, so we expect a few with small numbers, but half? It's easy to see that real estate is an easy career for people to choose—minimal cost to start, easy to get hired, and most call it an easy path to riches. Because the bar to entry is so low, few of these new Realtors come with goals or an action plan for success. For the young Realtors who may be reading this, here's what I think a solid starting plan for success looks like in real estate:

1. Host two open houses per week or 100 per year. Averaging four buyers through each open house means 400 potential buyers.

Two-thirds of people who come through an open house will buy or sell within one year—that's 260 probable purchases in the next twelve months.

2.   Hand-deliver invitations to the open house to forty neighbors before each event.

3.   Call your top twenty contacts weekly for referrals. Statistics show the average person knows six people they can influence who will buy or sell a house this year.

4.   Ask for referrals at each closing.

5.   Routinely preview listings in areas where you do a lot of business and leave a card each time. This increases the chance of the owners calling you when that house doesn't sell.

6.   Call withdrawn and expired listings.

7.   Start marketing in a "farm area." Send postcards and put up door hangers. Know the local numbers. Choose the neighborhood carefully. Be strategic about staying visible to all the neighbors.

8.   Hold an initial open house for each listing in your farm area to meet neighbors. This increases the likelihood the neighbors will list with you in the future.

9.   Use social media to consistently get your message in front of people.

10. Look for people or businesses who can give you multiple referrals—onsite agents, divorce attorneys, and corporate relocation officers. Cast a wide net!

In case you're wondering, none of this is all that creative, and anyone can discover most of it if they bother to look. Real estate isn't all about numbers, despite what some people say. However, until you have relationships bringing business to you, the numbers are an effective way to start.

In another area, I want happy employees. Let's say a situation arises, like the housing crash of 2008 or the lockdowns in 2020. These disrupt the workflow and peoples' lives, making them miserable. If I see my people unhappy, what quantifiable actions can I take to improve employee morale?

First, I need a baseline. I need to know how my people feel right now. Some will be a fairly happy, while some will be very unhappy. Some will be unhappy about pay cuts due to lower income. Some will be unhappy about coming back to the office after working remotely. The possibilities can go on and on. So I might create a survey, pass it around, hope people respond honestly, and read what they write.

Second, I verify. People sometimes write what they think the boss wants to hear. In a personal interview, people tend to speak more of what they feel. After I know what they feel isn't working, I put on them part of the responsibility for the solution. I ask them what changes they would make to bring morale up. I listen! I make notes! I discuss the ups and downs of what they suggest. I invest time with each of them.

Third, I implement. I might do it myself or I might get a couple of employees to take on this task and a couple others to take on that task. I give them a tentative goal, a tentative schedule, a tentative budget, and then say, "Go for it!" I'll also decide what constitutes success. Let's say, overall, my employees are incredibly unhappy and think our office is a 4 of 10. My goal might be an overall 6 or 8 of 10. (A 10 of 10 turnaround would be unrealistic, but I might go for that in the second year or third.) I might also have a high turnover that I want to cut in half. The goals depend on the circumstances.

Fourth, we review. I might send around another survey after six months. I may have more interviews, individually or as a group. We'll look at the projects I've handed off and talk about what's working and what isn't.

Finally, we'll adjust. We'll do more of what's working and less of what isn't. We may have come up with new ideas, and we'll try them. We may see stuff not working, and we'll quit them. We may have to take harsh measures and let a few people go. If we need to hire new people, we'll do that.

At the end of the year, a "final" evaluation—with final in quotes because this isn't the end. When we know how we've done, that becomes the baseline for new goals for the following year. Being intentional will bring about the needed change.

It's Never Too Late to Change What You're Doing

Make Family, then Other Groups, Your Priority

About 60 years ago, as I write this, I was born into a good family. Mom's gone on now, but Dad's still around, as are my siblings and other extended family. About 30 years ago, I created a new family with Janiene, and we have two children, one grandchild, and more of those to come, we hope. Someday, Dad will join Mom and, sometime later, Janiene and I will move on, but our family will remain. In fact, long after all of us have gone on, new members will take our places, but the family will remain.

In sharp contrast, in about five years, I'll hit the traditional retirement age and we'll make changes. The real estate industry has been very good to us, but it will be time to reach for other goals in my Life Pie.

I've mentioned people who had tremendous success in business or other pursuits but paid the price of a strong family. I repeat that warning. Nothing you do in life will be as valuable to you, as satisfying, or bring you more joy than what you do within the walls of your home. Make your family your first priority; make it clear to every business partner or associate that family comes first. Either they will respect you for it and respect that priority or you'll see they're people that maybe, you don't want to do business with at all.

If the family hasn't been your top priority, if your relationship with your spouse or children needs work, do the work. It'll take time, there may be some failures along the way but, in the end, you'll never regret that effort. If you doubt it can happen, don't. Have faith in yourself. Thousands, maybe millions, of people have made that same mistake and fixed it. The actions required to start to make the change you are looking to achieve are typically much smaller than you might think.

Embrace Your New, Intentional Life

I grew up in a loving, very close family—we express love for each other regularly; we celebrate our successes; we call and text. I know people who didn't and don't and I know that they are the majority these days. If that's your family situation, you can choose to change it. That choice and the actions that follow are intentional. Also, not acting is intentional, it's a choice. Whether or not they respond is on them. Whether or not you take a chance and try is on you.

If you're not being intentional about having the best life, you are, by default, intentionally not having the best life you can. That's true in family, business, and every other aspect.

It takes planning—your one-year goals and action plan—and some effort on your part in each of your five Life Pie slices. As you formulate those goals and plans, ask yourself: "If I fast forward to the end of twelve months, what would make me feel good about what I've accomplished in this slice, this year?"

When you decide that you're going to make the change toward exceptional results, an unimaginable life, and generational change, you have to go in with an attitude that says, "I'm done! The old way has not worked, and I now have a better way." That is embracing your new life with intention.

You're not going to take this on if you feel it's a bunch of fairy dust that you don't honestly believe in and can commit to. You're going to do it because it sounds and feels like the right thing to do. You have to embrace the idea, saying honestly, "I'm excited for the results." You also need to be honest with yourself about the mistakes you've made in the past, and more importantly, make a plan for the future.

You have to look at the Life Pie and it has to be important enough to you that you look at it every day, following through on the action things that you said would make your year better. That's a key thought, to **make** your life better, not just **hope** that it gets better.

Here's the difference between belief and faith—in any arena, not just religion—belief sits between your ears and does nothing. If you have real faith that you can accomplish something, you get off your butt and work at it. You act. If you don't feel motivated to act, you have no faith in the program and you don't embrace the intentional life.

If you write it down in a pie chart then put the chart into a drawer and forget which drawer it's in, you've changed nothing. Well, not precisely: You've changed one thing. You've told yourself there's a better way, there are things I'd like to accomplish, but they're not important enough to me, or I'm not capable of them or I'm not adult enough to step up or I'm not disciplined enough to make them happen.

Excuses abound and they're a sad commentary on you and another weight you're going to carry around.

That's why you have to embrace the change—wholeheartedly, enthusiastically, honestly. You deserve to live your best life, and that happens with intention.

Thrive Everywhere with No Regrets

Looking back on that guy in Florida, he built the second part of his life based on not repeating the mistakes he made during the first part. That's a good plan, but it only works if you let go of the past. Regret is sorrow or remorse or a sense of loss over past events or actions. Those feelings get you nothing, except to rob you of the happiness you have after fixing the mistakes that caused the regret.

That fellow built a second family to replace the one he lost. He should enjoy his life with them. Maybe, he can eventually build a good relationship with his older children and his former wife. We hope so, but any time he spends regretting how the early part of his life turned out, is time he can't spend fixing those problems.

My recent bodybuilding attempt took time away from other things, and based on how I expected to look, I failed. Should I regret putting in the effort? No, I really wanted to see if I could still compete at age 58. If it becomes important enough to make it to my Life Pie again, I'll be trying it one more time in the next few years to see if I can look better. There is a book *Failing Forward* by John C. Maxwell, which does a great job explaining how your failures help propel you ever closer to success. And the most successful people have long lists of failures—just look up Abraham Lincoln. It's a continuation of my need to keep my body in top shape. When I'm 75 or 85, I may have to deal with health problems like any old guy. I doubt I'll be posing for the judges. I don't want to look back and say, "I should've tried while I could. Now, I'll never know if I could've."

Suppose I decided that I wanted to get out on the track and race cars. Not professionally, just to see how well I can do it and to experience the thrill. That's something I could do now, in my 60s, that (again) I probably won't be able to do ten or twenty years down the road—pun intended.

If it's something that you're enthusiastic about, why not give it a try? Add it to your Life Pie, put in some time and effort, take pride in what you're trying to do and do it the best you can, then, walk away with the memories. Pay attention to your passions and you won't mind putting out some effort to do it well. Some poet once said, "Of all the words of tongue or pen, the saddest are, 'It might have been'."

That's a pretty good warning.

Examples of Potential Life Pie Slices

Community. That may include friends (your social life), your church congregation, clubs or associations, neighbors, and anything else that connects you to people outside the family.

Creative. Do you paint, sculpt, cook, collect stamps or coins, sing, act, build scenery, or plant a garden? Any hobby that brings you joy and brings beauty into the world is a creative act. Spend time nurturing it and sharing it.

Family. Your parents and siblings form your first family; your spouse and children are your second; your extended family is always there as well. Building and maintaining a strong relationship with each other doesn't just happen, especially as we grow up and add new slices to the pie. Each relationship must get individual attention to remain strong.

Financial. Work is where the money comes from, finance is where it goes. You have expenses to meet—really short-term goals. You have a vacation you're dreaming of—mid-range goals. You have a retirement to plan—long-range goals. You'll also have to deal with emergencies sooner or later—be prepared or risk being overwhelmed.

Home. Maintaining a house is easy, it's brick or stick and carpet and furniture. Maintaining a home is not; it's activities and memories and a place of refuge from the world.

Learning. As a Realtor, like with most professionals, I have to complete continuing education credits to keep my license. Outside of that situation, we all need to keep learning. They say the brain is like a muscle, it needs exercise. They're right.

Personal. "Me time" always sounds pretty silly when I hear it, but it isn't. You need time alone to read, meditate, pray, think, or just shut the world out and relax.

Play. Have fun! It's necessary for good physical and mental health.

Spouse/Significant Other. You've agreed to (ideally) share your whole life with one person. They need to be your second-highest priority, after your own well-being. They have a right to your time, your full and undivided attention when needed, and to your respect at all times. They also have a right to a little romance and adventure now and then—and so do you.

Work. Whether you're a "professional" or a "tradesman" or a "laborer," you owe your employer your best effort every minute on the job. You also owe yourself (and your family) preparation every day for that next, better job.

Once again, don't try to focus on everything all the time. Doing too much is as bad as doing too little. Review your long-term and short-term goals regularly. Think about your priorities and understand that they will change over time. Your Life Pie will keep you honest about what it takes for you to be successful in those most important parts of your life.

And, remember, it really is **_never too late_** to change!

CHAPTER 4

Family

I cannot repeat this often enough: For so many who are driven to be successful, family time suffers most often and most severely. Sacrificing family time is easiest because:

- Many don't even believe there is another option.
- It's easier than trying to strike a proper balance.
- Too many spouses and children are too forgiving of the sacrifices you ask them to make.
- Too many companies and others in our culture just expect it.

This has to change if the family is to remain the cornerstone of a strong society, of lives filled with exceptional results and generational change. No worldly or professional success can compensate for the loss of a family. No unimaginable life includes failure in the home. Jobs come and go; families should be generational–even forever.

Regardless of where you are or the mistakes you've made in the past, choose to change and be intentional and almost any mistake can be corrected.

Wife

Speaking as a husband, I've learned several ways to make my wife a priority. Each couple will be different but, once again, start this process by considering what would make me and my wife feel great about our relationship one year from now. If your goal is letting her know how much you love her:

- Tell her that you've set the goal. Remember that goals must be "quantifiable"–at the end of the year, only she can tell you if you've succeeded.
- Make it a point to tell her daily that you love her.

- Send occasional text messages just to let her know you're thinking about her and to remind her how important she is to you.
- Schedule a date night, at a minimum, once a month—preferably, once a week.
- Bring flowers home randomly once a month. It doesn't need to be a huge bouquet or a room full of roses, just a small handful is enough. Which flowers are her favorite?
- Be intentional about spending time together. In addition to date nights, plan an occasional weekend for two and an annual vacation as a couple.

Those are the easy-to-quantify activities. Some are less quantifiable but no less important. Let her know, by your overall attitude and actions, that your relationship with her is the most important aspect of your family.

- Talk through your issues. Never yell, don't even raise your voice, and no silent treatments. Don't go to bed angry. It's amazing how things improve when you have a calm, rational discussion, always remembering that winning an argument is a loss for your relationship. Together, you will determine the best path forward.
- Counsel with her about your goals and all major decisions. Learn to detect those decisions which are that important to her and support her. (Among our goals, we plan to remain in our present home for the next ten years or more. That's Janiene's choice. She loves the house. And even though we're empty-nesters and have more space than we need, she wants to keep it because of the memories associated with it and the memories that will be made there with grandkids in the future. In time, taxes and upkeep may be more money than we need to be spending, but it makes her happy, so I agree. A goal that requires no real effort is a great goal to have!)
- Which leads to my next piece of advice: never start a meaningless disagreement. If I have Mexican food for lunch and I come home to a wife who wants Mexican food for dinner, fine—we eat Mexican. She wants to keep our house, fine—we can afford it, it's not a burden. On the other hand, if there are critical issues, we will arrive at our decision together through calm conversation.

Questions & Answers

Does your spouse or partner need to work to meet the *family's* needs and wants? You, then, have to support them so that they can do that job while fulfilling their obligations at home.

Does your spouse or partner *want* to work to meet *their* needs and wants? You, then, have to support them so that they can live that part of their unimaginable life while fulfilling their obligations at home.

Either would be one of your principal obligations as a loving partner.

If your family doesn't need the income, you might encourage them to seek part-time instead of full-time employment. If you have children at home, you might encourage them to seek remote instead of in-office work or part time while the children are in school. Compromise is vital to success in most situations. If either you or your spouse ever get the idea that you need to "win" or to be "in charge," both of you should be looking for a lawyer– you're going to need them. It's a partnership–not a 50-50 partnership but a 100-100 partnership. Both of you need to be 100 percent committed to success.

Husband

The fundamentals are the same, even though the details will be different. He is your highest priority, make sure he knows it and feels it.

Children

Early on in my career, shortly after our first child–our son Cam–was born, there were times that I needed a reminder. Janiene would say, "I know you're here, but I really don't think you're here with us." Sadly, my response was, "Wow, that's so true."

With all the other things that were going on, I let my family's priority drop. Therefore, I had to retrain myself, to change that behavior. It doesn't do any good to simply be away from work, I needed to stop having work on my mind, which is where my mind usually was. I was not focusing on maintaining the proper balance. "So, really," I thought, "I'm getting no credit for anything, right? I'm failing them."

The fundamental rule is the same as everything else—be intentional:

- Schedule family dinners consistently and put them on the calendar. You probably won't be there every night but treat it like a business appointment—change the plan only when no other option is available.
- Make your children's events and family events a priority. Be there for games, recitals, or whatever, more often than not. Think of them as equally important as meetings with major clients.
- Coach the kids' sports or mentor them in other activities. Even if you're an assistant, even if you don't know much about what they're doing, you can learn the basics and you can help. If your work schedule doesn't permit you to be a formal part of their team, schedule time to practice with them at home in evenings or on weekends. It really is about the time together, and that happens when you're intentional.
- Schedule a regular family night—movie, family games, sporting event, museum, county/state fair. As long as the kids want to do it, it doesn't matter what you do—but strike a balance among fun, educational, and other activities. Also, occasionally spending time with the kids to give your spouse a night off is great. When the kids were young, I took them out one night a week so Janiene could have an evening at home to relax. It was a fun time for us and a much-needed break for her.
- When you're with them, be completely with them. Don't think about work. You shouldn't think about the family when you're in a meeting with a client; it's the same thinking in the opposite direction—except that your family should be much more important to you than that client.

Life Lesson Through Sports

One of my top priorities for the kids was building confidence—teaching them how capable they could be. Your family's goals and the way you reach them will be unique to you. For my family, that came through sports. I mentioned before that I coached my children's teams in every sport they played. That led to a couple of incidents which clearly showed me that they got the message:

Cam plays Baseball

When my son was 16, he played in an 18-and-under baseball tournament with his travel team, the idea being to help our boys improve by playing against better, older competition. Cam had been working with my buddy, a former pro ball player, on his pitching; moving foot position on the rubber, changing arm slot, and how to throw his best curve ball. I watched as he taught Cam to start his curveball right at the batter's head. Cam and I had been working on this for days leading up to the tournament and I found that the first time he would try to throw his curveball, it had no break. If he threw it a second time in a row, however, it had a really nice break and drop.

So, we were at the bottom of the last inning, with Cam's team facing a much better team comprised mostly of seniors. Most of them had just graduated high school; nine of their players had already signed to play with colleges. We were ahead by a run as we went into the last inning, and Cam was on the mound. With two outs, the other team's clean-up hitter—a 6-foot, 220-pound, 18-year-old—was at the plate against my 5-foot 8-inch, 150-pound, 16-year-old.

With two strikes, I motioned from the stands for him to throw his curveball. As was the case when we practiced, he threw the curveball right at the batter's head and it didn't break, forcing the batter to drop to the ground to avoid getting hit. He got up glaring at Cam, looking like he was ready to start one of those bench-clearing brawls you see in the major leagues.

Cam looked back up into the stands and I signaled for him to throw the curveball again. Cam nodded to me which, based on the size of the kid at the plate, spoke volumes about his confidence.

He threw his curveball straight at the kid's head again. Once again, the batter dropped to the dirt to get out of the way of the ball, but this time—just as it happened in practice, it broke and fell on the second pitch—right into the strike zone. "Strike three!" yelled the umpire and the game was over! (And the crowd went **wild**!)

Honestly, they were a much better team than Cam's and we were lucky to come away with the win. But how the game ended was not luck; it was the result of solid coaching and sticking to a plan. Being there to foster moments like this for my kids is what gave them the confidence that they can have high-level success in whatever they do.

Kailey plays Basketball

When my daughter was very young, she played three-on-three basketball on a half-court. I taught her to do a crossover–outside the three-point line, where they couldn't defend, she would dribble with her right hand with a closed left hand, then she would look at her left hand, as her reminder to open it. She'd pass the ball to her left and, as soon as the opposing player moved to Kailey's left, she shot her ball back to her right hand and moved to her right, going to the basket unchallenged to make a lay-up. That was her magic. She became very confident with "her move", and it gave her a whole new level of confidence that she carried through the rest of her years playing basketball. We still see that confidence today, in most areas of her life, and she still remembers how we worked together to make her stand out.

Well, years later, in a game I was coaching, we had a girl on the other team who was incredibly aggressive. In fact, she was pinching Kailey's teammates under the basket. This problem child was picking on every one of my girls, all of whom were close to tears. I mean to say that this was seriously freaking out our girls, who were just 11 and 12 years old. This, I thought, was ridiculous. Well, you can imagine how proud I was in our next huddle when we discussed what was happening and Kailey piped up, unsolicited, and said, "I got her."

The next thing I knew, she was underneath the basket with the bully, throwing elbows, and pushing that girl around until she complained to her coach that Kailey was too aggressive. Of course, all we did was take a page right out of that girl's playbook and turn it back on her. That girl was completely checked out because she couldn't take it, and that took her completely out of the game. I'm not advocating making young girls get tough with each other, but the confidence to stand up for yourself or your friends is something I wanted my kids to have.

This was a huge confidence builder for Kailey, for her to stand up and say, "I got her," and then prove that she, indeed, had her!

Today

Our children are grown and on their own. Cam has his own family, a wife and child, and lives nearby, but we still have to work intentionally, to maintain our close relationship. It's a bit more challenging with Kailey, who lives three and a half hours away, but we do the best we can and are still very involved in her and her husband's lives. We're intentional and we stick to the plan.

Janiene watches our 15-month-old grandson on Mondays and Tuesdays. It's great that I get to see my son at drop-off time and at pick-up time each evening—I make it a point to be home as much as possible. If we know his wife is busy doing things when he comes to pick him up in the evening, then we'll sit and catch up. Sometimes, we talk business, sometimes, we talk family, and sometimes, we just talk about whatever's on our minds. I've made it clear to Cam and Kailey through my actions that they can talk to me about anything. This is a trust I cherish.

Mom & Dad

Eight Years of Thursdays in San Antonio

Again, start with the end in mind. Ask yourself, "What would make you feel like this was a great year for your relationship with your parents?" You can put several things in your family slice of the Life Pie:

- Be intentional—tell them you love them every time you talk to them.
- Add regular phone calls and trips to see them to your calendar.
- Send them family pictures—formal portraits from school and casual pics of days at the beach or at the game or sitting around the table. With cameras in our phones and instant messaging, there's no excuse.
- Include them in your life—when you have major decisions to make, ask their advice. You don't have to take it, but you should respect them and honor them enough to ask.
- When you talk to them, ask about their past and present.
- Every now and then, send them a gift for no reason other than to show them you care. Maybe a dinner delivered from their favorite restaurant. If they say they're having a tough time finding something, find it for them online and have it delivered to their house.
- Encourage all family members, especially the grandchildren, to be intentional about giving them attention.
- If it's possible, be the one to initiate a family trip where the entire extended family gets together.

In preparing this book, I looked back over the time I spent with Dad and Mom. Meeting weekly for many meals, I've spent considerable time with them, now just him, over the last eight years. As a result, Dad and I have become great friends, maybe best friends. I've learned so much more about his life when he was young. We've even driven past many of the old places where he would hang out when he was a kid. This is something that could never have occurred had I not been intentional about scheduling and hosting time together.

Being intentional about the things in my Life Pie offers so much more than what you see on the front side. My relationship with Dad is a result of a simple decision of making my parents a priority for me as they got older. And that has evolved into something far beyond what I thought it could become. That is one of the surprise benefits of being intentional about living your best, balanced life.

What's Really Important?

You hear all the time of athletes or others who grew up with nothing and say their goal is, "One day, I want to buy my mother a house. We grew up with nothing, so I want my mom to have a good house." The likelihood of them ever playing a professional sport and having enough money to buy their mother a house is very remote.

If, instead, they picked up the phone a couple of times a week and called their moms or dads and said, "Hey, I was just thinking of you. Thanks for everything you did. I know how hard it was for you to be my mom/my dad. I love you." Or, maybe a quick text message that says, "Just thinking about you, Mom/Dad. I love you. Hope you have a great day." That would change their world more than a house. Years ago, I heard, "The greatest of good intentions pales when compared to the smallest of good deeds." Being intentional will keep you from forgetting those small, good deeds.

In some families, I think the most common mistake dads—as well as brothers and sons—make these days is taking the attitude that they're exclusively the provider. They also need to be nurturers and companions and show their love for their mothers, sisters, and daughters. Men are **all** these things, but only if they demonstrate it.

Speaking of a common mistake, I'd wager that your parents like to tell stories. If they do, let me ask, have you recorded them? Video, if possible, audio is good enough, but get Mom and Dad on the record while you can. Today, Dad is 90; our grandson might know him slightly. His younger siblings and the cousins we hope for may never even meet him. But they can know him, after a fashion, if they have recordings of him talking about his life. With Mom gone, Dad's memories and our memories of her are all they'll have.

I strongly recommend sitting down with everyone in previous generations, interviewing them about their lives, getting their memories on the record. Preserve those records along with the memories you're now making in some sort of family archive that everyone can access, add to, and enjoy. It'll take planning, time and effort but, 20 years down the road, you'll thank heaven that you did it.

Family Time

What's the key to friendship? I'd say that you like to be around that person even if you're not doing anything, you just hang out. One vital cornerstone of a solid family is that same desire to hang out with each other—like best friends, but even closer. Major family feuds and even small disagreements can alienate people so they don't want anything to do with each other. Pick almost any argument you want; I'll bet two family members somewhere have had that argument and sworn they'll never speak to the other relative again. Well, I had a disagreement like that, except it was with a friend. It was serious and we were (I'll be polite) "very heated" about it.

So, some years later, I decided to get rid of the baggage I had been carrying around as a result of that issue. I told him just one thing, "It takes two people to argue and I want you to know that, for my part, I'm sorry; and, for your part, I forgive you." He just couldn't say enough positive things. "I'm sorry. I'm so sorry it worked out like that, I feel horrible. I've always felt bad about it. Thank you, I should have called you."

It's the response we all hope for in that situation, but one we don't always get, right? But his response wasn't the point, from that day forward, *I* no longer carried any baggage about it. It was completely gone. Waking up the next day, I felt lighter, happier, and so, "Wow!" about life. I'd had a lot of emotion tied up in that event. Today, I have none.

Trips, Events, Attention to Family Issues

Mom and Dad set a splendid example in the big family trip they'd organize every year for all of their children and grandchildren. There are three of us, an older sister, myself, and a younger brother. We had great times as a family when we were young and, later, with the grandkids. My sister and her husband have three, we have two, and my brother and his wife have two. So, altogether, they had to orchestrate those trips around fifteen schedules. Well, they made it work, every year for twelve years I think.

It was incredibly intentional.

My parents would set these trips up far in advance to get commitment from everyone. Then they'd do all the booking and all of the other stuff—the heavy lifting—to make sure that it was easy for us. For parents with young children, it was really cool not to have to worry about that. As a result, my children have amazing relationships with their cousins. In addition, we'd go to Vail, Colorado, every year and the cousins would all hang out together. The trips were my parents' way of keeping the family remarkably close despite living far apart. Those family vacations were, in a nutshell, everything I've been talking about—a quantifiable goal, and intentional action, a focus on a Life Pie slice, creating a generational change, and so on.

Celebrations

Janiene and I take advantage of every opportunity to get our children home. We celebrate if either of them, or their spouses, has a birthday, received a promotion at work, or about anything else. We invite everybody to come, and we take them all out to dinner. If it's a holiday, we invite everybody to our house and we grill it up! Sometimes, we all get together down in San Antonio, and we grill out at Dad's place because that's what we used to do when the kids were growing up.

I know that most families can't do this much. That makes doing whatever you can all the more important. If your family is scattered across America, you can still take a half hour on your holidays—Memorial Day, Mothers and Fathers Days, Independence Day, Labor Day, or any old Sunday afternoon or evening—and have a video chat. Like my talks with my kids, it doesn't matter what you talk about as much as it matters that you do talk.

You can be passive, "Well, we'll see if they call and, if they call, maybe they'll want to do something." You won't, in the long run, be overly fond of what does not follow. People are busy, they need to be nudged, reminded, encouraged, even, to do the right thing. Eventually, it becomes a habit and automates itself somewhat, but habits can be broken—usually more quickly than they form.

Be the exception. Taking leftovers after everyone else has eaten their fill would be a terrible way to try and live. Food isn't the only nourishment you need; you also need the love and support of your family, and they need yours. Choose, then, to work for, and to provide freely, that support. That's how we obtain our unimaginable life.

Be There When You're There

I mentioned earlier that, early on, Janiene used to complain about my being mentally at work when I should've been home with my attention on my family. She was right, as usual, and I retrained myself away from that. I also wrote earlier of people who get so wrapped up in business that they neglect family. I wrote from experience. I was fortunate to have a wife that was always understanding. She didn't have to insist on her due portion of my time as husband and father, because it was a part of my Life Pie, which made me intentional about them.

These days, Janiene likes to end the day relaxed in bed with some TV time. I always have things that I could be doing, especially work things, but I've chosen to completely shut work down. Calls go to voicemail, to be dealt with at a later time. When I had a pager, years ago, I had a message on it, "This is Andy, leave a message at the beep and I'll call you back. If it's after six in the evening, it may be the next morning before I get back to you." I would then take my pager when I got home and tuck it under one cushion on the couch so I couldn't hear it or even hear the vibration. Now, it's second nature to be "with my family" when we are together.

At that point, I'm completely there with the family. My clients didn't know whether I had an appointment that kept me out until late or a family dinner to attend. They had no need to know. (Although, with the publication of this book, I'm kinda letting the cat out of that bag.) They simply knew I was unavailable to return messages until the next day. I will state, for the record, that no one ever got mad or threatened to fire me over having to wait a few hours for my response. Most of them, I assume, realized that they weren't my only clients, and getting a return call later was to be expected.

This practice made life easier in many ways. People who knew me stopped calling late at night. People who didn't know me didn't interrupt family time. I had their number and made sure I got back to them the next day, so they never felt ignored. My wife and, later, my children, saw that I was sacrificing business time for them—a practice they continue with their families in the next generation.

Make the Effort

I'm well aware that my family is the exception, not the rule. Many families get scattered, or maybe "splattered" is a better word to describe them. Families can just grow so far apart that you simply cease to be a priority to each other. That, by the way, can happen even if you all live in the same county—and, in Texas, counties can be very small.

If you look at people who live a very intentional life, you'll see them paying attention. They can take their situation then fast-forward to a later date and ask questions:

- "What would make me feel good about the family part of my life?"
- "What kind of change needs to happen to me to get what I want?"

Then, strategically, they plan to achieve that change. Anyone can do it; they only need to look at me, and many others who are living their dreams. We've done it, and we're pretty ordinary people; so they can do it too. We've experienced it and we've proven it can work, so, it's completely possible for you. Like everything else, there are techniques and those who follow them have the best chance of success.

It can be an amazing way to live, and lots of fun.

But there is a flip side to that coin. Once you understand that an intentional life can bring you success, you'll also realize that having a less-than-amazing life is also intentional because you have chosen not to do what's necessary. From the minute you know you can make that difference happen, it's not a choice to do it; it's a choice between doing it and not doing it. I've mentioned this before, but it's a critical part of taking control of your life and not allowing yourself to be a victim.

There's an old saying, "Indecision plus time equals a decision." Take our family vacations as an example. I could've received the invitation and decided, "Oh, I'll get around to this later." Well, later comes and my daughter has one thing going and my son has another and my wife has something else and I've agreed to do this or that and we just can't make it. Do that two or three years in a row and, if procrastination becomes a habit, we might've ended up never going.

The siblings might drift apart, the cousins might never become close friends, and Grandma and Grandpa might never get a visit in their old age because procrastination became a habit. It's happened so many times to so many people that I'd call it an epidemic of neglect. What's the saddest part of this situation? It's totally unnecessary; it should never happen, but it does.

That's the main reason I'm sharing these examples of what can be done. It's never too late to start and, although it might be difficult, making intentional changes can begin to change things immediately.

Of course, we also need to understand that we can't control other people. If "John Doe" becomes totally focused on work or other things, if the family suffers to the point where he and "Jane" get divorced and the little "Does" become estranged from Dad, "John" can still change and begin to recover those relationships. It doesn't need to start with big, showy gestures; in fact, it shouldn't. Trivial things, like a text or birthday card, are effective ways to start—just being intentional about showing that you remember them and cared enough to make contact. Let it grow naturally from there.

The other family members still need to accept his regret and his apology then give his efforts to change a chance to work. If they don't, that says a lot about them, and none of it is complimentary. If you're a "Jane" or a little "Doe," I encourage you to give "John" a chance. If his new attitude is fake, you'll figure that out pretty quickly. If not, you may cheat yourself out of a wonderful relationship that you would've come to cherish for the rest of your life.

CHAPTER 5

Spiritual

I believe in God, and "Spiritual" is and always has been, an important slice of my Life Pie. I respect your opinion, so it may not be among yours, and you may feel like you want to skip this chapter. But, before you do, let me please ask: might my spiritual journey have some value outside spirituality for you? I promise you it will. So I hope you will continue reading.

For those who share my view, let's look at this slice of the Life Pie exactly the way we look at all the others: fast forward one year from now. In thinking about your relationship with God, what would make you say, "This was a good year."?

While you're thinking about that question, think on this: many people who were regularly involved in church as children change when they move away from their parents' house. They hesitate or procrastinate or whatever you want to call it and they drift away from religious activity.

For many of those people, time passes and they begin to feel something is missing. After college or after they start a family, they start thinking, "I need to find a church and I need to go. I need to be part of something like that." Many of them then find a place where they feel comfortable, at least, and have a minimum standard that says, "I go to church on Sunday." Some take that standard and stick with it, enjoying the Sunday service, maybe an occasional weekday activity, and feel good about their relationship with God. Others take a more active role, volunteering to take part in the service, on committees, and other things.

An Investment

Like anything else in life, you get out of church what you put into it. If you drop by once in a while and sleep through every service, you may be wasting your time. If you go and listen with an ear to learning something that'll help you get through life better, if you make friends, if you take part in the activities, the church becomes a source of strength, growth, and joy.

Personally, church makes me feel more connected to God. I also feel the need to help people, to "pay it forward," as they say. Vincent is one example. He's enriched our family's life as much as we've enriched his. One thing about churches is that there's always someone in need so there are always opportunities to help.

If attending church weekly would make you feel better at the end of the year, then that goes into your Life Pie and transfers over to your goals and action plans.

Our time for church is scheduled, like family dinners and my kids' games when they were young. So, I reserve that time. I set no real estate appointments on Sunday until 2:00 p.m., period. My staff knows that, and because my business isn't a matter of life and death, things can always be figured out.

That gives us time to go to church then go out and eat after. I can get back to the house, get organized, and attack the afternoon, if there are things I need to handle or appointments I need to have. That doesn't always work; sometimes, other people's schedules have to control mine—that's business. But my relationship with God is far more than just attending church on Sunday.

I should mention that church is one of those things that's important to Janiene. She really enjoys going to services. That's an additional motivation and part of strengthening the family slice of the Life Pie. I value her above everything and attending church with her strengthens our relationship.

When I need some extra motivation, going with someone is motivating, even on those days when I'd like to stay home. Going out for a meal afterward with family or friends is also motivating. It's all tied together, and that works for me.

Mom

In addition to my Thursday trips to see Dad, I still visit Mom. She's interred in a mausoleum on the side of a small church at the cemetery. It's a

Catholic church and cemetery, so, after I visit her about fifteen minutes, I then go inside and kneel in the front row and just have a conversation with God.

I pray for about ten minutes. It's a quiet time each week when I'm completely alone with God. It's always good. Most of my conversation centers around my desire to live my life according to His will, whatever His will is. And to make sure I stay on that path. In the end, He knows what's best, so I'm not going to go and push for this outcome or that one. We talk, and I always ask Him to use me whenever He can.

At other times, driving in the car between appointments, I may have more casual conversations with God. I start by hitting the off button for the stereo. Generally, while driving, I listen to 1970s music, but when I'm feeling off, I turn the radio off and focus on talking to Him. I ask that if I can help people, please guide me to that person and help me know how I can help. Remember the words supposedly written by Ralph Waldo Emerson or Mahatma Ghandi or some other wise person:

> I shall pass this way but once; any good that I can do or any kindness I can show to any human being; let me do it now. Let me not defer nor neglect it, for I shall not pass this way again.
> —Unknown[3]

Likewise, if I'm facing a challenging conversation with anyone—business or personal—or I'm going to meet a client where there's a problem—and there are always plenty of those—I ask for help to do it right. By the time I get there, I am completely at peace. I don't have any agenda. I don't have any goal other than to be supportive and guide them to the answer that is in their best interest.

I believe that there is something beyond us, something watching out for us, and I believe that's a good thing for society. Even if there was no God, the moral code that religion has given us would be a better way to live than what much of the world is telling us these days. Ethics guide us, assisting us in avoiding bad decisions, helping us to think about

---

[3] Evidence points strongly toward Étienne de Grellet du Mabillier (commonly known as "Stephen de Grellet"), a 19th Century Quaker missionary, as the author. The statement isn't found in any of his works. The earliest known publication, which was anonymous, is in the Household Words: A Weekly Journal, 1859, four years after Grellet's death.

something other than ourselves. If you believe someone's watching you, and you believe this is something you should do or shouldn't do, you're much more likely to do it or to not do it. Or, to associate or to not associate with those who do.

My son ran into a situation like this. He had a couple of friends that he'd grown up with and I noticed that, when he was 16, he stopped hanging out with them.

"What's up with you?" I asked, "You haven't been hanging out with them for a while, right?" They'd been very close friends, teammates, and now, he seemed to have cut them out.

"They decided they didn't believe in God," he said. "Last time we were at the mall, the three of us, they started talking like, 'No one's going to see, let's just take it.' We're talking about stealing out of a store. And the feeling was, if no one is right here to catch us and tell our parents, what's the difference? What does it matter?"

I was enormously proud of Cam who, at 16, knew their lack of belief in God had changed their behavior, and he wasn't going to get caught with them doing things he knew were wrong.

Challenges

I think that most people in my generation were exposed to religion at some point in their lives. I also think part of my generation's problem lies in those who felt it was crammed down their throat, so they walked away.

The cool thing about religion, as I see it, is spirituality—your relationship with God. More so than what most people call "religion" today, meaning the church and its traditions or ceremonies.

The other cool thing about religion is its open nature. When you come back to it as an adult, if you've been away, you're there because you want to be there and people welcome you.

As a kid, I was an altar boy at Catholic masses. I'd ring the chimes, though it wasn't my favorite thing as I much preferred being out playing sports. I served as an altar boy because my dad did the readings and he made my brother and me take part as well. When I got to college, I was among those many who didn't give a second thought to going to church on Sunday.

Janiene had a completely different experience. She grew up with no formal religion and no real belief—her family didn't go to church, didn't even talk about it. As an adult, she discovered the church and now has been an active member of a ladies' Bible Study for over seven years, and faith has become a big part of her life.

Our daughter, Kailey, by the way, never went through that. She's always been incredibly spiritual, even picked her school—Dallas Baptist University—as a result of her spirituality. That was hard for me to understand, frankly. DBU is a small school and I thought she'd have a better experience at a larger university. But she and Janiene made the right decision; it was a great fit for who she is.

Opportunities

I've heard it more times than I can count that if you're enthusiastic about something, you don't mind putting forth the effort to do it well. I agree and I would like to add that even if you're not driven or motivated to be the best at this or that, you can still take pride in what you do—enough pride to do it well. If you do your best, you're living life with no regrets—not like that guy from Florida with his second family. He was trying to make up for the life of regrets he had with his first family. What a burden to carry!

That advice includes every slice of your Life Pie. You want to live with no regrets. When I say, "no regrets," I'm talking about looking back over the last five or ten years and being burdened by saying, "Oh, I should've done this," or "Oh, I should've spent more time with these people."

If you watch the news, you see stories about wealthy people who set up foundations and give their money away. Most of us don't get so rich that we can retire and spend the rest of our lives just deciding who we can help. Does that mean we can't do anything? Of course, not.

Many wealthy people give because they can; some may feel a need to be seen as philanthropists; some may do it because they get tax deductions. But I believe that most people truly and honestly want to help. For most, giving requires sacrifice—we have to give up something we want in order to help someone else—maybe it's a family member, maybe a friend, maybe a total stranger, like Vincent was when we met.

You can't do that unless you are paying attention to what's going on around you. I saw Vincent and I saw a need. My heart said, "Help him." It took my head a while to catch up, but it did catch up and I acted. As I've mentioned, this led to a great friendship. Even if it had not, I don't regret taking that first step of helping someone in need.

That's why I include charity in the spiritual slice of the pie. When we understand that we're all God's children, that we all need help at times, and that we all have opportunities to help, recognizing those opportunities to assist others becomes even more rewarding for us than for them.

That is the essence of the intentional life and the path to the unimaginable life. Live so that ten or twenty years down the road, you will have no regrets. Make helping others an intentional part of your life. Gary Keller told us in that first meeting years ago, that we were allowed to create our own perfect lives; we just had to work to support them. I can't name anyone I've ever known who was generous with their time or talents and regretted it. A lot of people I know counted their service as a great growing experience.

I know a man who lost his business in the COVID lockdowns. He started volunteering at his local food bank because the volunteers took home a package and he needed the food. As time passed, he found new work and rebuilt his finances, but he kept volunteering at the food bank, even long past the time he needed the help. Some of the food went to his relatives, some to his neighbors, and, sometimes, he just handed the food to his pastor and said, "For anyone who needs it," never knowing where it went.

That's a god-like approach to life or real humanity or whatever you want to call it—the attitude all of us should aspire to hold. For anyone else, that's real humanity—a real effort to care for others. It's also an example to our children and others: "If you can do it," they'll say to themselves, "then, I can do it, too, and I should."

Now, there's another lesson in the story of a friend who had such challenges with his work. Because he hadn't been introduced to the Life Pie, and thus wasn't as intentional about other important parts of his life, his family connections were also cut off. And since his spiritual life was severely limited because he could not attend his church and be part of that fellowship that he loved, it felt as though everything was collapsing at the same time.

The basic premise of this book and the reason it's called *The 80 Percent Project*, rests on getting the support you need from other parts of your life when one slice gets shaky. My friend was desperate because he didn't understand the importance of being intentional with all the parts of his life that he felt were important. This can happen. It can feel like multiple parts of your life can go all to hell at a time! How do you deal with that?

For my friend, community service filled the gap. He looked at his needs and looked around and found the support he needed in an opportunity to help others. Instead of focusing on his struggles, he chose to focus on helping others with their struggles, something that met his spiritual needs. He leaned into his belief that it is better to give than to receive, making new friends among the volunteers.

As you move through life, this will happen. School will be a slice for a time, probably to be replaced by work or career. That will, eventually, be replaced by retirement. You know these changes are coming and if you're making five- to ten-year goals, you can prepare by selecting opportunities that fit in with those changes. If life throws you a curve ball and you have to duck to get out of its way, you go down, but you don't have to stay there. Flat on your face might be a position none of us like to be in, but it's a new point of view. What can you see down there that you couldn't see when you were standing up? How can you profit (or help others profit) from what you see down there?

So, why are you still sitting there? Get up and get to work!

CHAPTER 6

Personal

Broad Strokes

The idea behind the personal slice of the Life Pie is simple: Like everything else, look twelve months down the road, and ask: "What would make me feel like I did well for myself during the last year?"

You could say, "Well, personally, I'd love to have a stronger or closer or friendlier relationship with this person or that person," and that's perfectly legitimate. That goal may also fall into the family slice or the work slice category, depending on the nature of the relationship. It's still personal because you're doing it for yourself. Personal goals generally focus on one of two end results:

- Self-improvement—changing something about you for the better. You want to change something about the way you are or do things; something you want to be able to do better consistently.
- Accomplishment—you have a specific event, achievement, or activity to complete. This might be something you intend to do several times but have had trouble starting, or something you want to do once, just to feel the thrill of it.

By the way, instead of calling it the "personal" slice, you may choose to split it into two:

- A "lifestyle" slice, setting goals related to health, eating habits, and fitness.
- A "self-improvement" slice, setting goals that relate to education or skills or experience.

Once again, you're not limited to my five slices. You can choose whatever categories you feel need improvement and you can have four or six or some other number, as long as you can give each part the time and attention they deserve. I encourage the 80 Percenters I coach to use five pieces for their first year using the life pie. By year two, they tend to have a much better feel for whether they need to expand their pie beyond five pieces. For my life, five has been the right number for me to live with no regrets.

Self-improvement

For example, let's say you choose a self-improvement slice. You could look at your life and decide, "I enjoyed reading, so I'm going to read twenty-four new books this year." Suppose, instead, you've always dreamed of a trip to Germany. Your self-improvement slice might include, "I'm going to study German this year so that by the time I leave for Germany, I'll be 'conversational.'" Once the trip to Germany appears on your life pie, one of the action items you create for that trip would be to become more familiar with the language., This allows you to put it in a spot on your calendar that affords plenty of time for you to accomplish the goal.

Accomplishment

Perhaps your bucket list says, "I want to run a marathon." Great goal but according to legend, after the battle of Marathon in Greece, a messenger ran the 26 miles back to his city to announce the victory and then died of exhaustion on the spot. Not a good plan. You'll want to train for a year, maybe more, just to get to the point where you can run that distance.

First, you need a full physical check-up so that you know you don't have any physical conditions that would make it dangerous for you to pursue this goal. Second, you have to start small. You have to start by running a mile or two, whatever you're comfortable with, then work your way up incrementally to the full race.

You break down the big goal into smaller, more manageable pieces. I'm going to run this far these weeks, then train myself to run farther and farther each week or month until 26 miles is possible. Then you work on speed. Putting this timeline on your calendar ensures you stay on your schedule. As is almost always the case with your Life Pie goals, the action items required to reach those goals are moved to your calendar.

For most of us, personal goals are the ones that scratch that specific itch each of us have, usually something you've been thinking about for a while but have never taken action on. Once it makes it to your Life Pie, your intention becomes a reality, complete with an action plan, timeline, and quantifiable end goal.

Anything can Fit Here

Well, maybe not "anything" because that's quite a lot, but the possibilities for personal growth and improvement are so broad; it's a little overwhelming. There are so many ways in which we can make our individual lives better and at the same time, help others. We're really cheating ourselves if we don't take advantage of one or two.

"I love animals so I'll volunteer at an animal shelter for a half day a week this year."

"I love animals so I'm putting a contribution to an animal shelter in my budget."

It could also be helping out at a women's shelter, volunteering to help children learn to read, doing some gardening at a city park, whatever floats your boat. Likewise, any challenge you're physically or mentally capable of completing is great.

"I'd like to climb Mount Ranier."

It's a good goal, especially if you start with something more manageable.

"I'd like to drive a pro-style race car or an old steam locomotive."

There are a few places in the USA that will give you some training and let you get out on the track or tracks and do that under proper supervision. Frankly, it can be something purely for fun.

"I want to visit Yellowstone National Park." "I want to see the Statue of Liberty."

"I want to drive old Route 66."

"I want to attend Comic Con in San Diego." "I want to see AC/DC in concert."

Maybe even the iconic or cliché, "I'm going to Disneyland!"

As I said, this starts with a vision of your life twelve months down the road, and a question: "What would make me feel like I did well for myself during the last year?" I hope by now you can easily see how being intentional about more than your business will change your entire life.

A Personal Goal of Mine: Compete After 32 Years

The great thing about being purposeful in life and living with intention is living the life you choose to live.

As I've written, I was a competitive bodybuilder in my 20s. That was before I got married and had children, so my kids never saw me that way, except in pictures. Well, I loved that life (32 years ago, as I write this), and the kids said, many times while growing up, "Oh, yeah, that stinks that we didn't ever get to see you compete because that all happened before we were here."

So I made the decision. To make a memory my family could take part in, I decided that I wanted to get back on stage.

Diet

I screwed up this one big time. I started off just as I had in my 20s with six meals a day of chicken for protein and rice for carbs, plus supplements to be sure I got all the nutrients I needed each day. And my chicken was to be extremely clean; to have no flavor, no seasoning, nothing. Just straight, boiled chicken because boiling chicken gets all the fat out of it. Well, the truth is, fifty-something bodies and twenty-something bodies shouldn't eat the same way. I got terrible heartburn, and I was miserable. Toward the end, I even had to tell my assistant Cecelia to answer all questions for clients other than for thirty minutes after I'd eaten carbs. I would never normally think like that but I wasn't thinking clearly. I wasn't feeding my brain because toward the end of the diet, I was eating so few carbs.

It got so bad that one day, while I was in the gym with my son, I started to pass out just after finishing a set of press-downs. Fortunately, he was there to catch me. I was having cramps all over. It was a miserable experience. But the goal was to get on stage and I wouldn't go on stage in less than the best shape I could be in, and that meant this diet, or so I thought.

I finally got smart and called a dietician for a consultation. She gave me some much-needed guidance on what to eat and how to prepare for competition. If I do decide to go back on stage and compete again, which I've considered, I'm going to bring in the dietician on day one and follow her advice!

You've all heard the phrase 'Knowledge is power;' well, it's true. Whatever you choose as your goals, as I learned the hard way, you can't just "Go for it!" You need to go about it the smart way.

The Workout Partner

Your partner is someone to hold you accountable. When I was young, I believed I needed to train every day for two hours in order to get my body looking its best. Having someone who knew my routine and was there every day with me, pushing me, was a guarantee that I would get my best workouts. As I got older, getting up at 5:00 a.m. was necessary to get my workout in and do the rest of the stuff I needed to do each day. Knowing that someone else would be at the gym and looking for me and would be calling or texting, asking where I was becomes a motivation for me to get to the gym. Once we were there, he was a great motivation to really push ourselves and do what needed to be done. As an added benefit, he was also training for the same show (different age group). Since this was his first time competing, having a training partner was equally important for him.

Let's go with an example you can probably relate to more easily: suppose you set a goal to take a two-mile walk every morning. You do this all summer and fall and it takes about forty-five minutes. Great, but then winter comes, and the weather goes foul and you don't want to spend forty-five minutes in the rain or snow early in the morning. So, you buy a stationary bike. You don't have to get up and get dressed and get out in the weather; you just walk into whatever room the machine is in and start spinning. After a couple of weeks, you decide you don't enjoy it as much as walking outside, but it's better than freezing your vitals off in sub-zero weather.

Spring has come, as it always does, and it's still chilly and rains some days. You just keep biking even though there are days when the weather's nice enough to get out and walk. Why get all dressed up when you can pedal happily in your pajamas? If you had a walking partner, that's why! Someone working on the same or similar goals, who will, as I said, hold you accountable with no corners cut. If I decide to hit the stage again, I'd hire a coach who really knew the business better than I did and who could talk to me about the smallest details of my body and how it should work.

The Show

So now here I am, 32 years later, at age 58, and we're off to Arizona to compete—Janiene and our kids with their spouses. Everybody is there to experience dad competing. They still talk about that vacation, saying things like, "Oh, man, my dad's still a bodybuilder!" They think that's a cool thing. I can't control what they thought about me competing, but I can control how I react to what they think. That makes this personal. Since they thought it was cool and wanted to be part of the experience, that made it family. That was a great bonus to stepping back on stage.

I entered two competitions. I won one of them and placed sixth in the other—that sixth was disappointing, because of my expectation. Now, the fact of the matter is, I didn't deserve to be any better. The way that I mishandled the diet and other things, I deserved to be where I was. However, knowing that I deserved no better didn't help my attitude. It was a big disappointment for me; because I'm so competitive. My expectation was that I would look like I did last time I was on stage 32 years ago.

But when I looked at the other guys around me, I thought, "Man, if I had been able to figure this out, I could have won the show." Next time, if there is one, I will.

My failure to win doesn't mean the trip was a failure. I left part of my goal in the "undone" file, but the family had a great time. They all saw me on stage competing. That's a win. That's a memory we'll share, as a family, forever. And because it was on my Life Pie, I did it after all those years of thinking about it.

Motivation, Discipline, & Strategy

Now, a question you might be asking: "Were your wife and children what motivated you to take this shot at competing after three decades?"

I'd say they helped motivate me. I wouldn't say they were the driving force. As I've said, I'm extremely competitive. So I looked out there and thought, "You know what, I think I can still get on stage and have an expectation of winning when I walk on." Now, whether that's right or wrong, who knows, but that was my thinking. The fact that my family wanted to see me do it was a bonus. I don't know if I would have done it solely for them.

You go through a lot to be able to compete on that level and it's a tremendous sacrifice of other things in life. You have to compartmentalize, to block out time and do the right things to be able to get everything done each day.

That's another reason to have a partner. When the alarm goes off at five and you hit it, you might despise your life at that moment. You might think, "Man, I would much rather sleep in." You might even have good reasons to do that. "Oh, I feel a little bit of a headache coming on," or "Oh, I think my knee hurts a little bit this morning. I better just sleep in and take the morning off." That kind of thinking is really easy and it's getting easier every year! But if you have someone counting on you in a partnership, you have a bigger reason to do whatever it is you planned to do.

In a separate example, suppose you are a single man in your 40s or 50s. By chance, you meet a woman on social media who attended your high school. She knew you but, at that time, was not interested in you even though you were interested in her. You're both single. After some time getting re-acquainted, she mentions she's coming to your city on business or a vacation. You suggest lunch or dinner to catch up and she agrees. Now, you have a problem. She's aged gracefully but your hairline has moved to the next county and you're no longer the slim 150-pound guy she knew way back then. Chances are, you'll be at the bike shop the next day checking out something you can ride around the neighborhood for an hour every evening or doing a quick internet search for the nearest gym that offers private coaching.

Is that a good motivation? If you achieve your goal to lose 20 or 30 pounds and tone up, will you keep it up after her visit? That depends on how you feel when you look in the mirror. An outside factor—family, job, friends, relatives, a bad report from your last physical—can be very motivating in the short term. It'll be up to you and you alone to decide if that's reason enough to keep it up after that short-term reason has expired.

Discipline plus Success equals Confidence

Everything you do, if it meets or gets you closer to your goal, is a success. Every time you're disciplined enough to get out of bed and go to the gym, or whatever your goal happens to be, you get a shot of what doctors call the "feel-good hormones"—dopamine, endorphins, oxytocin, or serotonin.

I'm not a doctor. I don't know how these things work, but they work. Do things that make your body react with those and your body will want more of them. That makes it easier to make the effort next time because even though your body is tired, you can remember the feeling you get from those hormones.

You also build confidence. When I started in real estate, I saw a bunch of ordinary people doing ordinary things and being successful. I'm not a genius, and I'm not a superhero. I'm an ordinary guy, just like they were. If they could do ordinary things and be successful, I could do more of those ordinary things and be more successful. That was my simple plan of action and it worked. So I did more of it and was more successful.

Every time I succeeded, it was a proof that I could and that my plan was working. So, I just kept at it and became a Keller-Williams top producer. That isn't to say everything always worked. I took promising ideas from others; some worked for me and some didn't. I recently saw a postcard that another Realtor was sending out. It was almost a carbon copy of mine. I chuckled because I'd tried a lot of different postcard styles before I found one that succeeded for me. I'm not even sure how many but she saw mine, liked it, and copied it. Smart move on her part doing what another successful person had already done.

Delete the Victim Mentality

Mostly, we are victims of our own perceived limitations.

I think if there is one trait or characteristic that does more damage to people than anything else. It is thinking that you're a victim. That is, allowing yourself to think of yourself as a victim. When I was growing up and something bad happened, Dad's answer was "You go figure a way out of it. Write down your three best ways out of it. Pick the one you think is the best and go for it with 100 percent of your effort. If, a week down the road, you look up and see that another answer was the better answer, you've already cleared the hurdle and you're moving down the road or you can abandon your first plan and try the better one.

To me, that was brilliant. Rather than sitting and stewing over it, do something! Get moving toward a solution. If you then find a better solution, change. I have friends whom I have known for a long time. This is the thing that's held them back in life. They don't proactively work at solving problems.

This idea that you're a victim—which means that someone else has control over your situation—also means they don't look at life and say, "That's amazing!" People who can look at life and see how amazing it is are the people who've figured out how to do it.

Control How You See Things in Life

Express some faith in yourself and say, "I'm a smart person. I can figure out how to do this."

If you're in an amazing relationship with someone you love with all your heart, then acknowledge that you and your partner will have problems. Decide now that you'll figure out a way to solve those problems. You have friends to give advice, a million books on relationships, your spiritual leaders, professional counselors, and—now get this clear—every single one of them wants you two to succeed as a couple! How can you fail with all those people to help, and all of both your families (we hope) praying that you'll succeed?

If you and your partner are living the intentional life, you two can figure out whatever is going wrong and figure out how to get through it. Those problems, and you know this, can be health, infidelity, loss of employment or career, trouble with the children or not having any children, and a million other things. You have each other and you have a support network available. You also have God. Even if you don't believe in Him, He believes in you. And, even for unbelievers, miracles do happen.

Suppose, instead, you haven't yet found that match. That means someone is out there for you. You might sink into a feeling of, "Wow, it must be nice. Wish I had somebody. I don't know if that's ever going to happen to me." If that's your mindset, then it's most likely that it won't. It's cliché to say, "If you think you can or you think you can't, you're right!" It's cliché, but it's true. We are our own worst enemies when it comes to motivation. If you believe the world is against you or assume it will mistreat you, you'll focus on the negatives. This mindset can turn you into someone no one wants to date, work with, or be around because of your attitude.

Instead, say, "My person is out there. I have to do what will put me near him or her."

- I have to decide what kind of person I want to have as my lifelong companion. That may include religious beliefs, political leanings, child-rearing doctrines, health and fitness plan, or any of a hundred other things.
- I need to go to places where that kind of person spends time. That may be business, church, clubs and associations, friends of friends, and more.
- I'm going to make myself attractive to other people—I'll dress well, speak and act politely, and be knowledgeable about the connection I want to build so we have something to talk about. I'll be someone that my special someone will find interesting and attractive.

You have to decide, "I know the relationship that I want exists—in premise. Now, I'm going to do what I need to do to prove that the premise was true. For next year, I may then set a goal like: "I'm going to four places each month where I might connect to a person that fits my goal for a mate."

For the next year, you're now waking up and thinking, "Hey, I'm going to spin class" or "Hey, some friends and I are going to a concert" or "Hey, I'm taking a trip to a ranch to learn to ride a horse."

A positive attitude says, "Whatever it takes is what I'm going to do."

And it goes without saying (so, I'm going to say it) that this advice works in business as well. "I'm going to associate with rising stars in my company" or "I'm going to volunteer for a special project at work" or "I'm going to add two software certifications so I'm more valuable to the company." That's so much better than sitting at your desk and saying, "Wow, she's so lucky to get that promotion. I wish I'd get one."

Luck rarely has anything to do with success.

Last Word

Your health is probably the most important slice of your pie. If your body is healthy, your mind is sharper. Your health could likely be better with a few minor changes. As a 20-something, I worked hard–like a madman, some said–to have my best physique for the competition. That was the extreme, and I don't recommend it for anyone except those willing to let it control their whole life to a large degree. But, on the flip side of that coin, everyone can do better in taking care of themselves, and we should.

Too often, our health seems to move to the bottom of our list of priorities. For many of us, it's always something we will work on tomorrow, or next week, or next month, or next year. It's the reason fitness centers are typically packed in January and almost empty by March. Other things become more important and our health suffers. Even when our plan is to start working on our health next year, many don't have the discipline to keep exercising after a couple of months (or weeks, or days). If we set health goals in our Life Pie, make a timeline, and add an action plan to our calendar, we're more likely to stay on track. That goes to the heart of what *The 80 Percent Project* is all about. If you improve your situation–physically, mentally, spiritually, familially–you'll have tremendous strength to call on when business, a relationship, or something else goes wrong.

CHAPTER 7

Work

Follow Someone Else's Success

In whatever industry, field, or position you're in, especially among the lower echelons of a company, there are always people who've gone before. Look them up and ask, "So, what made you successful in this job? What are your priorities and pitfalls?"

Some people question the ethics or appropriateness of asking your superiors about the quickest way to move forward. I don't see any problem with that, especially if you approach them correctly. Don't ask, "How can I make this job work for me?" Ask them, "How can I do the best for the company?" That shows you're a team player, not a maverick. If they want the same thing, and they should, they'll be happy to share, especially over a lunch you bought them.

I don't think it matters what company or line you're with; there's always somebody you can find who has figured out a path forward and advanced. Anyone who doesn't take advantage of that knowledge is cheating themselves and cheating their employers.

In a smart company, your manager should've assigned you a mentor—someone tasked to help you get oriented and off to a good start. If not, nothing says you can ask for help, and you should. They've been there, don't reinvent the wheel.

In addition to that (or instead of that, if you're an independent like a Realtor), you can still look around and watch what people are doing. Is it working for them? Can you adapt what they do to work for you? Is there any reason you shouldn't try? When I started in real estate, there were so many Realtors. It was pretty easy to look out and ask, "Okay, who's successful and how are they doing it?" Then, I did what they did.

When I decided I wanted to be more successful than they were, I did more of what they did. Eventually, I hired a coach to show me the fastest track to reaching the goals I set for myself. Looking back, the coaches in my life have been the single biggest factor in the pace at which my career has advanced. This holds true not just in business, but also in life. Knowing there are wildly successful people who figured out at some point in their journey that massive sacrifice isn't necessary to achieve your goals, should give you confidence that there is a system you can model that should provide you with similar results. And if at first, like me, you decide to be coached, that is available to you with as little effort as going online and signing up.

The work slice of my Life Pie is likely the piece that you need the least help understanding, as most of us are strategic about our work, given the fact that it's the biggest factor in determining our lifestyle. But for those of you who haven't figured out that working with goals is the easiest way to be able to reach your full potential in business…and in life, that may be the biggest lesson you can learn from this book. If you haven't worked with written, quantifiable goals before, and at the end of this book you decide to give goals a try, you will likely never live without them again. They are that impactful! And for those of you who use goals in your business life but haven't used a Life Pie and created goals for the other areas you determine to be most important in your life, I say be ready to see an immediate glimpse into what your future life can be. Because you will see changes so quickly, you will likely question how something so simple, which requires so little effort, hasn't been part of your life before. The answer is because, unlike me, you didn't have parents to model after, or coaches to guide you—until now. By living this balanced life, your children, their children, and the future generations will learn it through osmosis., And you will have been the catalyst for generational change in your family. How amazing is that? You have the ability to make life better for your family for generations to come.

Back in the 1970s, an investment firm ran a remarkably successful series of commercials:

> Good investments don't walk up and bite you on the bottom, and say, "We're here!" Finding them takes good, old-fashioned hard work—research, the kind they do at Smith Barney. Smith Barney is among a handful of investment firms singled out for

> their work and research. Smith Barney, they make money the old-fashioned way. They earn it!
>
> —John Houseman[4]

Is there a better way to succeed than hard work? Well, there's a joke based on that commercial: "We made money the **old** old-fashioned way—we **_inherited_** it." Clever, but not really an option for most of us, and those who do inherit wealth often misuse it, ending up with nothing because they never learned the value of money or the proper way to handle it. No, there isn't a better way.

I repeat, "copycatting" is the easiest way to quickly improve your position. Find someone who's successful and do as they do. We've done that over the years with all kinds of things. I like to say I've stolen from the best people in the industry.

It's also been done to me. As I mentioned earlier, in the neighborhood where I market, I send a specific type of postcard. I recently saw an almost identical postcard by someone else. It's a compliment, a testimonial to the fact that my system worked. It was brilliant on her part; frustrating, yes, because she may take business from me using my own methods, but still brilliant. Coming from the outside and looking in, I thought, "Smart person, that's the right answer." Will it work for that other Realtor? Not always. I copied a bunch of others before I found one that brought me the return I wanted. This other Realtor may find the same challenge.

The point is the learning curve. Every job has one but you can shorten that curve by imitation. My son-in-law just started a new position at a new company. The first thing he did was visit someone who'd been in his position and recently moved up. He asked, "What's your advice for me? What should I be doing?" That guy was more than happy to help, "Oh, man," he said, "great question. Here's what you need to do." Right there, my son-in-law had it figured out. It worked, by the way. He moved up to the next level very quickly. For the rest of his life, my son-in-law knows as he goes into a new position, he won't have to figure it all out by himself.

Where life balance is concerned, I know the path. I've lived it, as has my family. This is why this book should interest you—because we're in the

---

[4] Ogilvy & Mather, a unit of the WPP Group, 1979. https://www.youtube.com/watch?v=yAMRXqQXemU, accessed 24 July 2024.

same life, essentially. The details will differ for everyone, but the same strategy applies for all of us:

- Listen to those who came before—in the case of this book, that someone happens to be me.
- Move in circles where you can meet people who can mentor you. Network with like-minded professionals, political activists, church members, hobbyists, athletes—you name it.
- Get yourself that mentor or coach, maybe several—a life coach (like myself) to assist with personal development; a health coach to guide you through changes in diet and exercise required as you age; a spiritual coach to help you develop your relationship with God; and so on. For each slice in your Life Pie, you may need a different coach. I believe this is so important that I have all these coaches available in my coaching business.

Compete by Setting Goals

Getting ahead professionally is a goal most people set. The definition of "getting ahead" varies among people as much as their career choices vary. For some, it's owning their own business; for others, it's retiring at age 45 or 50 instead of 65 or 70; for others still, it's climbing the corporate ladder.

Realistically, how long does it take?

An Example

Again, think strategically: If the view from the top of the corporate ladder is your dream, you need to ask, "How long does it take for someone to get from the 'entry-level' through the management and executive levels to a C-suite position?"

Let's say you're an accountant, newly hired into a large business. You see the chief financial officer (CFO) and you realize that he's not more talented or more intelligent than you, but he is more experienced than you and has a broader skill set. You need to catch up to where he is. How do you do that?

Expected Skills in a CFO

I took a look around the internet and found several skills expected in a CFO. Notice that many don't directly involve money:

- Business—how to think critically and solve problems—decision-making, innovation and adaptability, negotiation, strategic planning.
- Certification—depending on the company, the CFO might need to be a certified public accountant (CPA), Chartered Financial Analyst (CFA), Certified Financial Fiduciary (CFF), Financial Risk Manager (FRM), or hold other licenses or qualifications.
- Communications—how to influence and persuade, how to present, to write, to speak in public.
- Education—many have masters and doctoral degrees and earn continuing education credits.
- Ethical standards—honesty, reliability, trustworthiness are vital when handling other people's money.
- Finance—accounting, regulatory compliance, investments, stocks, risk management.
- Leadership—goalsetting, emotional intelligence, supervision, training.

Experience

Smaller businesses generally require less experience in their applicants, making a CFO position in a small business a potential steppingstone to the C-suite in larger businesses. Major corporations might expect candidates to have 12 or 15 years in management jobs to be considered. That, however, is not an absolute:

At age 29, I achieved what others deemed improbable, at least. I became CIO and Director of Information Management for the Queensland Department of Tourism, Sport, and Racing. I proudly held the title of the youngest CIO in the Queensland government. Despite peers who were decades older, ***my unique mindset, drive, and unwavering focus propelled me forward***. Recognition arrived in the form of the Premier's Leadership Excellence Award for my contributions to the government in 2000.

> So, how did the shy kid from India reach an executive role in a conservative Australian region at 29? ***I differentiated myself from other candidates***. I could see the organizations were struggling with the changes they needed to make, so, I had to find a way to drive change. This meant reprograming my thoughts, rewiring my neural networks, and challenging self-imposed limitations. I cast aside the shackles of conformity and embraced a mindset that sought new possibilities, always creating value for stakeholders. Reflection, self-exploration, and a relentless pursuit of personal growth became my guiding principles. As my perspective expanded, so did the opportunities that lay before me. Thus, through the power of mental metamorphosis, I defied the norm and blazed a trail to manifest my grand aspirations to serve others.
>
> —Kumar R. Parakala (emphasis added)[5]

Joining the C-suite before 30 is rare but not impossible—if you have the resume that qualifies you.

That first list is relatively easy. Many companies offer employee training or contribute to advanced degrees and, if not, training is available through other sources. But how do I "differentiate" myself? Parakala writes, "I had to find a way to drive change. . . I cast aside the shackles of conformity. . . sought new possibilities. . . [with] a relentless pursuit of personal growth."

Exactly what I've been counseling: Living with intention created exceptional results that drove generational change and led him to an unimaginable life. Way to go, Kumar!

In a corporation or any other endeavor, the short answer is "do better" or "do more." As a Realtor, it's generally a question of selling more properties. As an employee, it's accepting additional assignments. It's looking for problems and finding solutions—especially good if you can do so before the boss is aware the problem exists. It's being noticeable in a positive way.

You can give in by saying, "Yeah, but they're smarter than me or better looking than me or they're willing to work harder or it's easy for them

---

[5] Kumar R. Parakala, *Lead to Disrupt: 7 Keys to Success in the Changing World.* Jersey City, NJ: Leaders Press, 2024.

to wake up or whatever." All false. Yes, there are a lot of very smart and exceptionally talented people out there–ignore that! They choose how hard they work and you choose how hard you work. If you do run into that rare "genius," ignore the fact. If you can't compete with them intellectually, you can still outwork them.

Deal with problems or hurdles you can overcome. They've set the example and shown me this is possible. So, go into action with a set of goals and a plan. Start with, "How many months or years will it take me to develop the skills that qualify me for that position?"

Okay, having that list, set a goal to acquire this skill over the next year. What skills will take three years? What skills will take five years or ten years? What else can I do over a year, three, five, to make myself valuable and "differentiated"? Company committees? Community service? Other employers?

If I can accomplish those goals, it will place me in this percentage among my coworkers. So, now I put it all on a timeline. I need goals that are written, quantifiable, challenging yet inspiring, realistic, and aligned with my values and ethics. Then, I need to meet those benchmarks.

Think Strategically but Develop a Plan of Action

My ten-year goal might be to become a finance executive in some company. My five-year might be to become a managing director. Whatever is going to require that you stretch (without rising on the corpses of your coworkers) is where you need to head. Now, I put together an action plan to meet those benchmarks:

- I need to complete this certification in one year.
- I need to complete this degree within three years.
- I need to move to this type of position in this type of company within four years to obtain this type of experience.
- I need to move to that type of position in that type of company in about year seven to obtain that type of experience.
- And so on, all the way to the C-suite.

Have a Mentor/Coach—Be a Mentor/Coach

Up front, I suggested going to someone who's more experienced to help you figure out how to do it. That's a mentor, plain and simple, nothing more complex. That shouldn't be your only discussion. If the individual is (or individuals are) willing, get together for lunch once a month. Talk about your job and their job. Learn how they advanced. Get their take on successful coworkers and how they achieved success.

Your mentors—yes, plural—should include a professional mentor; in our example, an older, more seasoned accountant who can help you navigate changes in the profession and get your certifications or other education. You also want to develop company-specific mentors who can introduce you to the people in the company (and other companies) who can advance your career. And, I repeat, you need a life coach, like myself, to help keep the 80 Percent Program in balance.

Now, you have, I assume, heard the old proverb, "Learn. Do. Teach." That's exceptional advice. A friend of mine once told me of his father's educational standard, "You don't understand it until you can explain it to someone else." Also, absolutely true. A preacher, back in the 19th century was asked a simple question, and his answer might surprise you:

> [I]s the principle of self-aggrandizement wrong? Should we seek our own good?

The preacher responded:

> It is a correct principle and may be indulged upon only one rule or plan—and that is to elevate, benefit and bless others first. **If you will elevate others, the very work itself will exalt you.** Upon no other plan can a man justly and permanently aggrandize himself.
>
> —Joseph Smith, Jr. (emphasis added)[6]

Notice the detail, "to elevate, benefit and **bless others first**." Developing a reputation for being the "go-to" person who's willing to help out wherever you can is like gold in the career bank, for two reasons: First,

---

[6] As recalled by Oliver B. Huntington in "Sayings of Joseph Smith," Young Women's Journal, Vol 2, Num 8, May 1891. Salt Lake City, Utah Territory: Young Ladies' Mutual Improvement Associations of Zion.

people will like you. Second, when you need help, you will have banked goodwill that others will want to repay.

There's also a third reason, a little gold deposited in your personal bank: When you go out and do something for someone else—something for which you get no reward beyond a warm feeling that you could more easily get by taking a hot bath—you become a better person.

That, too, gets noticed, and not just by coworkers.

Motivating Yourself

Most days as a Realtor include a lot of different things—phone calls, meetings, house showings, contracts, mail, whatever. How do you get and stay motivated? I suggest two possibilities.

Hurdles

I learned early on that I need to make my hardest calls first thing in the morning. I do that because if I don't, every other call that I make, or every other interaction I have, is jaded. In the back of my mind, I'm thinking, "Oh. geez, I got that call coming up and this client is very demanding and I don't know how the call's going to go, and so on." If I make my worst calls first thing in the morning, all of that anxiety is released., I dump all of the stress out and I feel the whole rest of the day goes more smoothly.

Because I'm excited. Everything else can be, "Wow, that's done! Let's go out and conquer the world! And by the way, those stressful calls never go as poorly as you think they will. It's human nature to go to the worst place and get all stressed out over (excuse the cliché), "a tempest in a teacup." By that, I mean, why am I getting stressed about this call if I worry that they'll want to go this direction or that? I give them my best professional advice, suggesting that this is the best way to proceed to sell their house. Then, if they go in another direction, well, it's their property. That's where your mind needs to be, but, until you make that call, you're probably thinking, "Oh, this is going to be awkward."

And if it is going to get awkward—and it does, once in a while—aren't you far better off addressing it? Because it will rarely be your absolute worst-case scenario. You're always playing it out in your mind as if it would be the worst case, and that's what makes it your worst call of the day.

It's tough, but it can be very motivating to just jump over the hurdle, then the next one, then the next one, and move on. You'll soon notice that each hurdle got a little shorter. That's motivating.

Momentum

While I was writing this book, I met a guy who does graphic design. We had an interesting discussion:

"Years ago, I was creating some teaching aids for American history classroom use. I wanted to do a poster of all the state flags. I thought to myself, 'Okay, this is fifty separate drawings and some are tremendously complex. They have a hundred or more different small elements. How do I keep myself motivated to get all the way to drawing number fifty?'

"I thought, 'Oh, the answer is simple: I'll do all the easy flags first, and I'll build my way up, like building a wall. I'm going to get to a point where I'm tired of this project, and think, 'This is too much work. I quit.' So, I made a bet with myself that I would be so far along that I was going to say to myself, 'No, you can't quit now, you're too close to being done.'"

Then he asked me to pick a number between one and fifty. When did I actually have that thought? I said, "Probably between thirty and forty."

"Close, forty-two."

"Wow," I said. "that's brilliant."

"Not brilliant, simple psychology! I completed forty-two flags and I was done, fed up, and I wanted to quit. But, I had just eight flags to go. What idiot quits with almost 90 percent of the project done?"

So, he didn't. He'd developed the momentum that carried him through those last, toughest drawings to the end.

Whether you start with the toughest parts and slide downhill or start with the easiest part and psyche yourself up to the hardest part, depends on you, your project, and other things. Do what works for you, but if dealing with the worst things first gives you peace throughout the rest of your day, and allows you to be your best self, I still say to attack the hardest things first.

Be Proactive

Whatever you do to keep motivated, you need to do it first.

As I've been coaching people in real estate, I keep telling them, "If your client calls you, you get no credit for that conversation."

If they have to call you first, it means they were sitting at home or at the office contemplating, "I wish I had an update on this. I wonder when this is going to happen." Well, an hour later, they think about it again. Later that day, again, and finally they think, "Hey, I just want to know, when are we doing that open house you mentioned a while ago? Is that still on? Haven't heard anything." That's reactive, not proactive; you get no credit for that call.

Instead, I call you and say, "Hey Jack, it's Andy. Hope I'm not bugging you."

You say, "No, I'm good."

"Hey, let me give you a quick update. Based on the feedback we've had from our showings thus far; I want to go another ten days. If we don't have it under contract in ten days, then I want to have a conversation about price. But I don't want to have the conversation now because my goal is to sell it in the next ten days. I feel like that'll have given it a fair shot at the original price."

You say, "Okay."

At the end of that conversation, you think, "Wow, that was impressive. He's really got this under control."

Now, if you call me first, and I explain it all to you just that way, it doesn't have the same impact. You're thinking, "I had to chase this guy down just to find out where we are."

Being strategic is a good plan, in large measure, but being proactive—taking the lead, going the extra mile—is a great plan.

Begin with the End in Mind

> Begin With the End in Mind is based on imagination—the ability to envision in your mind what you cannot at present see with your eyes. It is based on the principle that all things are created twice. There is a mental (first) creation, and a physical (second) creation. The physical creation follows the mental, just as a building follows a blueprint.
>
> If you don't make a conscious effort to visualize who you are and what you want in life, then you empower other people and circumstances to shape you and your life by default. It's about connecting again with your uniqueness and then defining the personal, moral, and ethical guidelines within which you can most happily express and fulfill yourself.
>
> —Stephen Richards Covey[7]

Also:

> Accountability breeds responsibility.
>
> —Stephen Richards Covey[8]

That designer's analogy is one I'd thought of myself. Design the wall; build it block by block; don't skimp on the mortar. Life usually is that simple, in theory. Most of the time, we hit rough spots, bumps on the road, whatever analogy you like to use. It happens—and we all know what *it* is. If you know your destination—like my designer friend with the flag poster—you know what you want to achieve.

If you're using *The 80 Percent Project* fully, you know how you'll feel when you reach the end of that task or project or that level of performance. You chose that project because of how you knew you'd feel when it was done. You also know that the task isn't the only thing in life, and

---

[7] Stephen R Covey, *The 7 Habits of Highly Effective People: Powerful Lessons in Personal Change.* New York City: Free Press (an imprint of Simon & Schuster), 1989.
[8] *Ibid.*

certainly isn't the most important thing in your life. Work is for the now; your family (nuclear and extended) can be forever. Friendships, likewise, can be forever. Every study that I've ever heard of has concluded that people with "the long view" have the advantage over those who focus on the here and now.

95

If you never sacrifice long-term happiness and joy for short-term fun or profit, work will be a means to an end, as it should be. Think of **you** in your "golden years":

Surrounded by generational change personified by your happy, successful children and grandchildren. Surrounded by friends, coworkers and others who've achieved exceptional results with your help. That's the legacy I intend to leave behind, my unimaginable life. It could be yours, too.

CHAPTER 8

Financial

Obviously, financial and work goals are intricately linked but they aren't the same. Speaking of your financial Life Pie slice, I'm thinking again of the long-term. Savings for your children's college education or a house or major vacation is part of it. Preparing for your retirement is another part of it. Investing, taxes, insurance, and everything else you spend money on—now or in the future—is part of your financial strategy.

Remember, we start with our long-term goals of ten years. Then break them down into five- and three-year mid-term goals, and finally, one-year short-term goals. I passionately believe that if you start thinking that way and act intelligently to reach those goals, it's a guarantee that you will make significant change for yourself financially.

That, of course, assumes that nothing disastrous, like a severe illness, injury, or major economic downturn happens. (Think 2008 or 2020, but don't think too hard or long or you'll have nightmares remembering them!) I recognize that some things are completely outside of my control. Even in those worst-case scenarios, you might be prevented from reaching your goal, but you'll be in better shape to deal with them than someone who's never prepared financially.

I've known people who are completely focused on finances, like some who are focused on work. Many who came from nothing are desperate to prevent going back to that situation. And, like Ebenezer Scrooge, go totally overboard. They may wind up incredibly wealthy—$10s of millions or even $100s of millions wealthy—but they're not happy. In their mind, they've done it for **you**, not for **themselves**, but they often end up alienating the ones they've been trying to protect. I repeat, "Discipline is trading what you want now for what you want most"—it's a true principle but, if you delay all your gratification for years and decades, you may find yourself so obsessed with saving and holding your wealth, you can't bring yourself to enjoy it.

Legacy

The American dream, according to many, is, "I am better off than my parents and my children will be better off than me." Simple, easily quantifiable, challenging and motivating—in all respects, a great goal.

Similarly, the "first great question" of American politics is, "Are you better off than you were four years ago?" That's a vital question to ask because politics, national and local, are going to impact your financial situation. The COVID-19 lockdown was a prime example for a number of reasons:

- Numerous businesses were forced to close. It is generally believed that about 40 percent of those businesses never reopened. Millions of jobs were lost.
- Millions who were near retirement and capable of retiring decided to retire early, even though they would've continued working had not the lockdowns occurred. Many later decided to return to the workforce and do something new, many have not.
- Changes in the way we work, such as the massive increase in remote work, changed how people work, opening some opportunities for many, closing some opportunities for others.

The uncertainty of future political policies makes keeping control over your finances all the more vital. That requires intentional action. So, what kind of financial legacy do I want to leave with the people you love?

The same questions, slightly rephrased from what we've been discussing, "Looking twenty or thirty or forty years down the road, what would make me feel good about what I've done?" (Hopefully, you'll live that long or even longer.) "What would make me feel like my life was a success?"

I've said that I have an extremely competitive personality, but I don't need to be the wealthiest guy in the world. My world is not about money. Money is a tool, like a hammer or a computer—nothing more, nothing less and it's helpful to look at money that way to be successful.

My Children

Among my long-term goals, (like most parents) I want to leave my kids in a better position than my parents leave me. Who doesn't?

I intend to leave my children a legacy, but it won't just be money. A better legacy is attitude, education, and confidence. Janiene and I have taught our children to be self-reliant, how to succeed, and to prioritize happiness. That's more valuable than any amount of money we could leave them. Aside from a knowledge of how to have a solid, lifelong relationship with their own families, it's the most important legacy we can leave them.

That's generational change! That's how families go from being incredibly poor, having nothing, to being wildly wealthy in four or five generations—or just a generation or two.

Living intentionally with an eye toward the unimaginable life will be an example your children see and, most often, embrace. Even if the parents have never read this book and don't specifically sit the children down and teach them these principles, the kids will know it by their parents' example. They'll have lived it right along with their parents. That's the normal course of human development. We live the life we saw with our parents because that's what we know, what's familiar, what's normal.

There's usually nothing wrong with that because most parents are good, honest people doing their best. In some families, that's not the case, and, if we're lucky enough as children or young adults, we're independent people with freedom to choose to continue or to change. You've probably heard a million little kids say, "You're not the boss of me!" It's like a mantra with them, every kid seems to know it and say it at some point. Well, mom and dad are, in fact, the boss, but, when you hit age 18, (in most things) you are officially the boss and your mantra should become, "Only I can choose or change my destiny."

That's a life-changing realization. That's the start of living with no regrets.

Closely related to that, we know how most people grew up. We know that a lot of parents do not have the resources to leave a legacy to their kids. Moreover, many will need their children to help support them in what turned out to be the not-so-golden years. The kids will never say "burden," but the parents probably will think it, even if no one ever says it. No parent will ever voluntarily be a burden to their children.

For some, there is no choice if illness or debility robs them of their independence, as my mother's Alzheimer's robbed her. She and my dad were fortunate that his health was—and remains (at age 90)— good enough that he was able to care for her during the last few years of her life. And he's still fine, living on his own. Should that ever change, my hope is to move him to Austin so I can be more involved in his daily life. (Maybe that's also why Janiene wants us empty-nesters—to keep our 8,000 square foot house!)

My Spouse and Myself

Doing better for my kids than my parents did for me means preparing for the possibility of my natural infirmity. That should be the primary motivation in your financial slice.

How do I get there? You need to break it down. The advice of a trained retirement planner can be valuable in answering this and related questions.

- When do I expect to retire?
- How long do I expect to live?
- How do I want to live?
- How much money do I need to fund that life?

The traditional age is still 65. I don't plan to retire then, I have too many things I still want to do. My plan is to work until I no longer enjoy it or until I can't do it, because I enjoy working. I don't enjoy sitting around. But 65 is as good a benchmark as any.

You should begin retirement planning as soon as you get your first job. Most young people don't know that because they were never taught how—or even that they should. Once again, whatever your age or situation, you can change. You can start planning today, and you should. The answers to those bullet-point questions are well known. If for example, you were born in 1959, you'll reach your 65th birthday in 2024, the year I write this. The life expectancy at birth (for all people) was sixty-seven years for a male, 73 for a female. Having reached age 65, with childhood illnesses, youthful accidents, and other factors behind you, guys should make it to 80, gals to 89. That's great, but here's the good news/bad news: Statistics mean nothing. They, the folks that put these lists together, are looking at the population as a whole. These numbers have no relationship to you as an individual. You, the 65-year-old male, may live to 67 or to 97, there's no way to tell.

The money you need is far easier to calculate. You need $X to live "comfortably" (you get to define that term) and, over the past 60 years, inflation has added $Y to that amount each year. It's safe to assume, therefore, that you'll need $Z every month to live "comfortably" in ten years, when you think you'll want to retire.

You, then, can have your financial people guide you where to invest, and in what amounts, to reach that goal.

The Community

I will mention, but just in passing, charity. If you choose to support your alma mater, local church, community center, library, museum or some animal sanctuary, that, too, takes planning. While you have an income, it's easy. You just put it in the budget. When you retire, you're no longer an income-producing entity. Although we hope your investments are earning interest or dividends, you are, fundamentally, an income-consuming entity. If you want to continue to support your favorite charities, that needs planning.

- Will you continue monthly or annual contributions?
- Will you designate a portion of your estate to that charity?
- Will your bequest be cash or stocks or bonds or property they can use or turn into cash?

This will form part of your legacy and must from day one—whenever you decide to include those organizations in your legacy—and discussed with your financial planners. The tax and other benefits can be attractive.

By the way, if you're a regular—especially, if you're a significant contributor, especially to a smaller charity—your charity needs to know your plans. If you switch from an annual contribution to a final bequest, they may not see it for years. They need and deserve to know now, so they can adjust their fundraising plans to accommodate your change in circumstances.

One final thought: If I've said I'm going to take my estate and contribute it to a charity when I pass, that, too, is a generational change. My children will see it and they will, I hope, apply that principle to their lives and it'll become part of their legacy.

Retirement

I've mentioned the financial aspects of retirement, but I want to end this chapter with a non-financial, but closely related, thought. In America, too many people plan to have a retirement but they don't plan what to do with retirement. I cannot stress enough the intentional nature of a life without regret.

Choose the life you live. Not just today, with work and family and community and so on, but later on, after retirement. Many head into retirement with things around the house that they've been putting off because of other commitments. From what I've seen with my clients, you don't want to start retirement with worries about big expenses. Schedule these updates in the years prior to your retirement, while your income is still strong enough to support the expense.

Want to travel? Want to try a new work endeavor? Want to learn new skills such as painting, gardening, playing an instrument or improving your singing? Why not? What's stopping you?

Poor planning.

Let me tell you a story: Many years ago, the activity director of an assisted living center called a tour bus company and suggested a tour for the residents—about 45 were ambulatory. The arrangements were made but, when the driver arrived, he was met by one very young, very enthusiastic activity director and forty-five surly seniors, most with canes or walkers, all acting like this was a trip to a torture chamber and they were the guests of dishonor!

During that first day, the driver took the opportunity to chat with some of the residents. Why were they going on the tour if they seemed so unhappy about it? "Well, we don't have anything else to do," was the basic response. The driver had a private chat with the activity director. He suggested that they get the old folks up early, get them moving and keep them moving until the sun went down. She agreed.

The plan took a couple of days to get up to full speed but, by the end of the tour, the residents were laughing, singing, and looking forward to next year's outing. By the way, when they returned home, they had their canes in the overhead racks and the walkers in the luggage bay. It was a tremendous success.

Sadly, the activity director transferred to another of the company's facilities a few months later, so the outing never happened. Three years went by, and the driver got curious. He really liked those people and wanted to check in on them. Sadly, over forty had passed away and those who were left were all bedridden.

The new activity director didn't understand living the unimaginable life, so she did things the way she'd seen others do it, with a few, simple, non-strenuous activities that never "pushed" the residents. She underestimated them, so they just faded away.

That is the life of regret—you stop trying and eventually, you just fade away.

CHAPTER 9

Generational Change

Kids' Lives and Generations to Come

For so many children, they didn't see their parents putting family first. They didn't hear, "I love you," they didn't see that the parents were taking care of them in a personal, individual way. Their parents didn't take vacation trips with them, didn't coach their teams, weren't there for their events. As we've discussed, most people follow the lead of their parents when it comes to raising their own children. So being intentional about getting it right can have profound consequences for generations to come.

You who were among those children, I assume your parents loved you and you were important to them. Maybe they didn't know how to show it. Maybe they got so caught up in providing for you or dealing with their own problems that they couldn't show it. So, instead of carrying on in your parents' traditions, many of you went in different directions, following your peer group, what you saw on TV or the movies or heard in your music, or you just drifted through much of your life.

A friend of mine, highly active in politics where he lives, keeps telling people, "Politicians are fond of declaring that they hope to take the government in a new (and unspecified) direction. Well, 'straight to hell' is usually a new direction, but not one to be desired."

He's right. If you want to change things for the better—and who among us doesn't want that for our children?— you first need to figure out what that new direction is and to be sure it's the right direction.

Fortunately, *The 80 Percent Project* and many others in businesses and religious or community organizations are willing and able to help. Life can be complex and frightening, but it doesn't have to be overwhelming. Wherever you are along the path, you can stop, look around, assess where you are against where you'd like to be, and find a path that will help you, and your next generations, to get there.

Learning through Osmosis

My daughter Kailey graduated from Dallas Baptist University, a small school in many respects. I was not a fan of her going to such a small school since my college experience was very different at a huge university. She and my wife convinced me it would be a good fit for her, and as has almost always been the case, Janiene was right. Kailey's freshman year at a smaller school created a great friend group of around fifteen kids.

One weekend, one of the Dallas kids invited everyone over to their family's home to hang out and use their pool. I got a call from Kailey after that weekend letting me know how her weekend went and thanking me for how she had grown up. She also had something surprising to say.

She was surprised by the reaction of the other kids to the home they visited. She said the kids were amazed that their friend had grown up in what they saw as a big house with a pool. What Kailey saw was a very normal house in a very average neighborhood, with a small pool in the backyard. She said she had no idea how differently she had grown up. To her, this friend's house was more of what she expected would be a starter home she might buy in her 20s as a recent college graduate.

My daughter wasn't raised as a little rich girl, and she wasn't being superior or conceited about her friend's home. We're successful and blessed, and both children know it. But this experience pointed out to her in a way she'd never really comprehended before. That children know what they know because they were brought up to it. The life they expect as adults is the life they lived in their early years. That weekend changed her thinking a little, as have many experiences since. Today, she's a confident, more experienced, wiser young woman who's working as an integral part of *The 80 Percent Project*. She and her husband have their beautiful, modest, starter home that they absolutely love; however, she believes that more, if desired, is absolutely obtainable with a plan and hard work. That's the important part of this story: she doesn't "need" more based on how or where she was raised., However, if she and her husband desire more as their family expands, she absolutely believes it possible!

Lost vs. Driven

I'd like to speak, as it were, directly to the next generation for a moment:

There are a couple of ways of dealing with challenges that I see other people employ. Some immediately get overwhelmed and can't recover because they don't see a pathway to success. They get lost in a foggy mental heaviness that causes them to feel, "Why does this kind of thing always happen to me?" Sometimes they see someone else having success and, internally, they look at that and say, "Wow, it must be nice, right?"

I don't understand that attitude because it never happened to me. I credit my parents, Dad specifically, whose mantra was, "See a problem, write down three solutions, then pick the one you think will work out best and go for it!" Dad was very pragmatic, as in the time he told me, "You're going to have a job on your 16th birthday." I needed to learn some things about life and living it like an adult, with a job and bills and taxes and all that, was his best solution to that problem.

It seems to have worked so far.

I recently watched a podcast of someone who's become highly successful in construction. He was talking about this exact subject, and I agreed with him wholeheartedly. When this gentleman sees someone else's success, he doesn't resent them for it. He gets excited because he knows that, if they've done it, then he can do it. He doesn't get lost in excuses or ignorance. He doesn't assume something is impossible just because he's never done it.

When challenges arise, you might need more information or some new skills to get the problem solved. But successful people are confident that they can find a solution to the problem. It's the whole "glass half empty" vs "glass half full" scenario. When faced with challenges, your options are two: (A) Look and see only that the glass is not full but do nothing about it. If you do, the whole victim mentality is watching you, pleased. (B) Step up and solve the problem.

With option A, you're lost. You may think "If I do nothing, I can't fail." Absolutely true, but you can never solve the problem that way.

With option B, if you act, you may fail. That won't be the first or last time you fail, I'd wager, and you may, through your failure(s), learn what doesn't work. Eventually, whittling away the possibilities until the correct solution becomes clear.

There's no time or circumstance in which it'll serve you to just sit in a chair and sulk. Dreadful things happen to all of us. When they do, even if you feel totally lost, take a good look around. Pick a direction and start walking. Eventually, you'll hit a road you can follow to wherever it is you're going.

Some of you were raised in a way that has left you lost when you start out as adults. Sadly, some parents, despite their best efforts, don't explain how the world works. A rare few never try. They haven't prepared you for the challenges you'll face. I'm sorry you had to go through that, but it is what it is, you have to deal with it and learn on your own what you didn't learn in childhood. Everybody hits adulthood missing a few key points, some miss most of them. Don't let yourselves become victims to what didn't happen.

Each generation, we hope, sees farther and does better by standing on the accomplishments of their parents and grandparents and so on. Whatever happened or didn't happen, you can still make it happen. You can still create generational change by not repeating their mistakes.

A Life Pie Success Story

Years ago, on one of our Disney cruises, it fell on me to make the reservations for the trip—a rare occurrence. As a novice booking flights, I booked our return from the cruise on a 4:30 flight. That seemed logical, thinking it would take some time to get from the ship to an airport almost two hours away by bus. Unfortunately, I misread the time we needed to be off the ship and on the bus for the airport—7:30 a.m.! You can imagine the love I felt from my family as we waited at Orlando Airport for over six hours.

My son was around 15 at the time and, in an effort to help fill the time, I introduced him to the Life Pie and helped him through the process of filling out his. Nothing else was ever said about it, just that one time to show him what it meant and how to use it. Honestly, it was less intentional on my part and more about filling time with something constructive. I never brought it up to Cam again, and he never mentioned it to me.

Fast forward to his first year of college. I got a call from him telling me about one of his baseball teammates. This fellow lacked direction; he had no idea what he was going to do after college. He also didn't understand how Cam had such a grasp on, and confidence about his future. I think Cam was equally surprised that his teammate wasn't confident about his own future. Cam proudly explained how cool it was for him to show this player how to use the Life Pie.

What? We hadn't mentioned the Life Pie since the cruise. I told him I was surprised that he remembered the conversation, and he informed me he had been using it ever since. Today, he's in software sales for a multinational company and in 2023 (his first full year with the company), he finished in the top one percent internationally, earning a trip to Hawaii for his family. All this at age 27!

Being strategic and intentional about your life leads to good things and instructing your children (and others) to be strategic and intentional gives them a huge advantage.

Lost in Misinformation and Disinformation

Since the information age began, we've added a tremendous amount of information made available to us. Most of it is wrong.

And millions of people get lost in that tidal wave of data. As one example, I'm now 60 years old, and everything I've ever contemplated putting in my mouth has been praised and condemned at some point in my life. Dairy products were criticized for decades, and numerous substitutes created. Now, there's in-depth research questioning whether those substitutes are as healthy as people claim they are. A vegetarian diet has long been advocated by many, but some now claim that we can, and should, get all our nutrition from meat. The list goes on. Sometimes, it's gone back and forth several times.

In politics, we may find the worst examples of too much knowledge (that is, opinion) and too little wisdom. I don't blame anybody for being confused or lost about who or what to vote for.

"Misinformation" is generated by people who, with the best intentions, get it wrong. Back in the 1950s, doctors actually said the human body can't run a mile in under four minutes, as the heart couldn't stand it. Roger Bannister proved them wrong, and now, every competitive mile runner does it.

"Disinformation" is generated by people who intend to deceive. Some of them do it with a straight face and credentials to back them up. Tobacco companies actually advertised the health benefits of smoking for decades, until a genuine medical research pointed out the health risks. Tobacco's risks are so serious and costly that every pack of cigarettes now carries a warning label.

Lawyers have a phrase worth memorizing: "Do your due diligence." (I have a friend who's rephrased that slightly, "A measured paranoia is a vital survival skill.") Don't trust people, advertisements, or speeches just because they sound truthful or appeal to your emotions. Do some research, find as many points of view as possible. Weigh the evidence carefully and choose your truths like your life depended on them.

It does.

Needy & Intimidated vs. Confident & Independent

As part of my research for this book, I got a copy of *Retirement Runway*, a truly short, particularly good book. Outwardly, it's about financial planning but, if you read it carefully, it's about generational change. It's a collection of short stories–grandpa (recently retired) explaining to his grandson (recent high school graduate) various aspects of retirement planning. In the last story, grandma takes over to add a little feminine wisdom. She shows her grandson a book of their family history:

> She gently shook her head, as she turned the pages, showed him photos [of her ancestors] stretching back over a century, and named names. "You're heir to more than what your parents or their parents have done for you. You're their heir, too. You've heard of Isaac Newton's famous phrase, 'If I have seen further [than others], it is by standing on the shoulders of giants'?"
>
> "Sure."

She spread her hands over the book, "These are your giants, you stand on their shoulders." "And on my shoulders stand my children and grand-children?"

–Joseph A. Clark[9]

Everything we do affects other people, bringing those others closer to success or to failure. As parents, we have the unique opportunity to help build our children's future by helping them discover how to answer fundamental questions of living. Some of which are:

- In what arenas will they face the world?
- How will they accomplish the dreams they choose?
- To what level of accomplishment will they rise?
- How well will they do in those arenas?

Those decisions will begin with their natural talents and gifts. Those talents and gifts are raw materials, like iron and coal. We, as parents, can forge those materials into quality steel by teaching our children to develop their gifts and by helping them understand how to answer those important questions of life.

Some will become steel in the girders of high-rise office buildings. Others will become nails and electrical wiring in family homes. Several will become works of art. Maybe a few will become cars, trucks, or bicycles. That part the children will decide.

You can't remake your children in your image or live the life you wanted through them. You can help them find out what's most important to them–their passions. You can help them learn what they're able to do well enough to earn a living–their skill sets.

Most importantly, you can teach them basic survival skills like cooking, sewing, and laundry; how to organize their time and money; how to research problems, find solutions, and get things done.

In short, you can teach them to go out into the world as capable adults.

---

[9] Joseph A. Clark, CFP. *Retirement Runway, A Story About Family and Legacy*. Jersey City, NJ: Leaders Press, 2024.

CHAPTER 10

Experiential not Theoretical

I developed *The 80 Percent Project* early on and have used it throughout my adult life. It's not a theory I came up with recently; it's been the method by which I built my unimaginable life. I am absolutely confident it can do the same for you. My family has also been using the program and they've also found success. With their permission, I share some of their successes as well as my own.

If It's Worth Doing, Do It Well

My son is now (in 2024) 28 and is, in his own words, "in his glory days era." We frequently reflect on all of the things we did as a father-son duo—especially now that he has a son of his own. He recently reminded me of something that happened when he was 18. Cam and I had a strategy for his first year playing college baseball that came about through the guidance of a great friend (and ex-professional baseball player), Kevin. He recommended that Cam not touch a bat, ball, or glove for the first two months of summer break. He'd give his body and mind a rest while still having one full month to prepare prior to the start of his freshman year.

Over the course of those two months, Cam's feeling towards baseball shifted from obligation to longing. He spent last month of summer energetically pouring himself back into the sport he loved, spending most mornings and afternoons on the field and in the batting cage.

Shortly after he arrived at school and met his college team, I got a call late that night from him: "Dad, we just had our first scrimmage against live pitching. Only two guys hit home runs…" To which I replied, "and…?" Cam quickly responded, "I hit three!"

This is *The 80 Percent Project* in a neat little package. Kevin didn't want Cam thinking his life revolved around baseball, so he forced him to focus on everything else for eight weeks. He returned to the game he loved with a rested body and new enthusiasm. "Do it well," doing the best you can do any activity, doesn't mean focusing your whole heart and soul and calendar on that activity. It means balancing that with the rest of your life. Cam took time away to reignite his passion for baseball and counted himself fortunate to have had a friend and mentor who knew that a passion can quickly turn into an obligation. We can do well at what we feel we must do, but we do our best when we do what we love.

Be Disciplined

Mom and Food

My mom, back in the day, placed third in the Miss San Antonio contest. She was 5-foot 2-inches and would frequently quote that old song lyric, "Five foot two, eyes of blue, oh, what those five feet can do!"[10]

For the entire time I was living at home, she always prepared dinners for the family—a meat, a vegetable, some kind of carb or starch, plus, on many nights, a salad. She always ate what we ate, but our meals were served on normal dinner plates while hers were typically served in a small bowl. As far back as I can remember, and certainly long before I was paying attention, she was disciplined about how much she ate and, other than pregnancies, never allowed her weight to get to 110 lbs. She was incredibly disciplined about the size of her portions because she wanted her cheesecake dessert. It would typically be the tiniest sliver of cheesecake, but it was always there—her cheesecake—in the fridge or freezer.

Mom was never big on traditional exercise but she and dad went dancing three nights a week for about thirty years, until Alzheimer's took over her life. Mostly, she controlled her weight and appearance by absolute discipline over the portions she ate. It was my first lesson (by example) of discipline.

---

[10] Music by Ray Henderson, lyrics by Sam M. Lewis & Joseph Widow Young, "Five Foot Two, Eyes of Blue (Has Anybody Seen My Girl?)." New York City: Leo Feist, Inc., 1925. (Original ukulele arrangement by May Singhi Breen.)

My Parents' Approach to Real Estate Investing

Dad retired from the Army at around 45 years of age, and they began investing in real estate. They started small, buying houses with notes that Mom worked to pay off as early as possible. She always sent more than was required on those monthly payments. They saved a huge amount on interest by adding just a few dollars to each monthly payment.

They also created a system that worked well for them and used it over and over again to grow their little rental "empire" to fifty houses, managing all of them themselves. They were efficient, using the same carpet and same color paint in all of them, making it easy for quick refreshes when a tenant moved out. They had fixed rules about how long it could take to do the "make-ready," and how quickly they needed to get it leased after it was ready to show.

Dad told me they never looked at prospective tenants' credit scores; they looked at stability as a guide to how long someone might stay with them. He looked for long stays with past landlords and long work histories with employers. He would call to verify both. If it was a couple renting the house, he paid attention to how long they had been together. He learned early on that. If they broke up, there was a high probability that neither would be able to afford the rent individually. When I had them on the radio show I did for many years, someone asked them why, with all of those houses, they hadn't moved to commercial or apartments, rather than deal with all of those houses.

Their answer was simple. "We have our system and never deviate from it, and we have no desire to learn a new way when this one works so well." Though their real estate investing took place after I had moved out on my own, their example was clear to me. Years later, I got a call from a real estate associate in San Antonio asking if I knew an investor who'd buy a portfolio of houses at sixty cents on the dollar. I immediately called my dad and asked if he and mom were interested. He replied, "If they're more than fifteen minutes from the house, they don't fit within our system and I'm not interested."

They created a detailed, orderly system that worked well for them and they had the discipline to never deviate from it. That's why they never burned out and continually grew their portfolio of houses right up until Mom started to get ill.

Be Grateful for Every Day

My parents were married for 65 years. Mom took the kids and followed him to all his military duty assignments. They raised three children, together. When he retired, they started a business and ran it together as full partners. They went dancing three times a week. They lived together, they worked together, they recreated together. They were as perfect a team as any two people I've ever met, and much more so than most.

Then, Alzheimer's hit her, and she started fading away. Dad sold all the rental houses. His life, for the last three years of hers, centered on caring for her. In fact, it was almost his exclusive occupation.

Her passing left a huge void in his life. His soldiers had moved on. Their business was gone. They'd given up their social life. They'd lost touch with all their old friends. You've heard of "survivor's guilt," well, I think Dad experienced something very much like that. Why, he asked, did God keep him around when he no longer had a purpose?

I could see and feel his struggle early on. But over time, the grief eased and he realized he was going to be around for a while, so he couldn't just give up on his life, even though it felt very empty.

He adjusted. He still had a sense of loss, but he created new routines. He restarted his daily *To Do* list. He became, once again, his old self, finding reasons to be grateful for each day.

Our weekly visits and meals became part of that new routine. During my visits, he often mentions how reading obituaries amazes him, especially when he sees the ages of those who have passed away. He now comments on how fortunate he is to still be here. He's come full circle from wondering why he was left without her to wondering why he's so lucky to still be alive and well passed age 90.

A tomorrow isn't promised to any of us. A tomorrow like today is promised to none of us. The days we have are a gift, and we should be grateful for each one. Start each of those days with gratitude and you're in a far better position to deal with the challenges that life will certainly throw our way.

Embrace Tough Times

Your competition will get weaker as you get stronger.

When Cam was around 10 years old, at the end of his regular Little League season, I asked him how he felt things went.

"Not very well," he replied.

When I asked him why he felt that way, he said that in the past seasons, he outworked everyone, getting lots of extra practice. Since he didn't do that this year, he felt his performance was very average.

I reminded him that he had two weeks before district play started and if it was important to him, he could do what he's done in the past and be ready to be his best for the first district game. Every single day for the next two weeks, Cam worked on his Hit Away batting trainer and pitched from the mound I made for him. At that first district game, Cam hit a home run on his first at bat and pitched the whole game, winning 6 to 1. He recently told me he thinks of that story almost every month as an adult because it had such a significant impact on how he does things since.

As part of the family slice of my Life Pie, I committed to being there for everything the kids did growing up. As a result, both have great memories of the things they learned from being coached by their dad. Those things, and the memories that go with them, are priceless!

Most Challenges can be Overcome, Some must be Endured

This example is very personal, a very hard season of our family's life but, to this day, it was the best decision I could have ever made to live a life with no regrets.

My mother started showing signs of Alzheimer's around 2014. We've always been a remarkably close family but Mom and Dad lived in San Antonio after his retirement and I've lived my adult life in Austin. Very close, but not so close that we saw each other every week.

After the diagnosis, I knew I needed to be more intentional in my life, prioritizing my parents more than ever before. As Mom began to decline, I watched Dad navigate the changes as he saw his wife of more than six decades become a vastly different person and his world become so much smaller. I knew I needed to step up as a son. In that time, it was not only the need to support Dad and love on Mom but, also, to prepare for her loss with no regret. Hard statement and a hard fact to live with, at that time, but it was the truth.

I quoted earlier a statement by a man who became a C-suite executive in a provincial (state) government at age 29 by differentiating himself from other candidates. I intended the slices of the Life Pie to help you differentiate and prioritize the various facets of your life. Making time with my parents a priority, putting them on my schedule every single week, became part of my family Life Pie slice. Not just to call them every day, which I did, but to physically be with them every single week. Once written down, it began.

It's more than eight years since I made that commitment. We lost Mom on 17 August 2022, but I still visit Dad every Thursday, leaving home at 6:30 a.m. and returning around 2:30 p.m. I still call each day, many days more than once. It's on my calendar and my office manager knows to schedule nothing for Thursdays before 3:00 p.m.

My dad, my hero, has become my best friend in these years. My intention in the beginning was to support the people that loved and raised me in their most challenging time, while also ensuring that Mom felt loved by me every day of her life. Now that she's gone, I have no regrets. She's at peace and my heart is at peace concerning her. My visits with Dad will continue until he joins Mom, that's non-negotiable.

I would've given anything, in addition to all that Dad and my siblings would've given, to have Mom free of that awful disease. To live the intentional life is to live with the understanding that "life is what happens while you're making other plans" and "what cannot be cured must be endured." That doesn't mean those challenges have to be entirely negative experiences.

Let me propose a question: "Did you do the best you could do?" If you can look back on your relationship with your parents, with your siblings or other relatives, or with anything else that you've ever done, and say, "Yes," then you're living a life without regret.

It's Never Too Late to Create Change

Earlier, I mentioned many successful years with my team of Realtors. With the shifting market of 2008 came a lot of questions for everyone in real estate. Our team had been winning national awards, but I could see that everything we'd known was about to change. Even with our success, there were a couple aspects of my team that I wasn't totally happy about during this run.

We seemed to have lost our presence in the luxury real estate market. I hadn't been selling for several years and really missed it. As we came out of the recession, I looked at how I might be doing business in the future. I saw an opportunity to shift back to luxury properties and start selling again myself. Considering the fact that I was already 17 years into my career, and had a model that was very effective, this would constitute a dramatic change. So, I looked at the immediate future: Sales down, several of my agents were ready for change and looking to create their own futures outside the team. The answer became clearer.

Change was inevitable even if I kept doing business as I was doing it back then, so I completely changed my model to get back into the luxury market. In hindsight, it was the right decision. I was able to shift to fewer homes sold with much higher commissions. And because I was back to selling myself, the bottom line was hugely different.

Was the post-recession realty world the reason for my change? No, the shifting market just gave me the nudge I needed to look at my options. I liked what I saw and, after 17 years of doing it one way, it became clear that there was a better way. Along the way, I proved to myself that it's never too late to change.

Do Not Play the Victim

In 2008, the Great Recession started and the housing industry got hit hard. As a family, we knew it was time to regroup. My wife Janiene was a stay-at-home Mom at the time but decided to start working. She began caring for Mary Jane, a young couple's six-week-old baby—the mother was Kailey's first-grade teacher. It brought in some additional money to our family (in what could be uncertain times ahead) and helped support a new family that was struggling with the hard decision of daycare. It was a win-win for both families. The plan was to care for Mary Jane for her first year and then see what other arrangements should be made. Janiene immediately embraced the new challenge. At that time, Cam was in middle school and Kailey was in elementary school, so, Janiene had to deal with two schools, no buses, and a newborn in tow—every morning and again every afternoon.

Sounded like a recipe for misery to me, but Janiene felt differently. It was a scary time with a lot of unknowns, but Janiene chose to lean into the wind and move forward boldly. She was contributing to our family, she was helping another family, and she woke up with purpose every day instead of worry.

The bursting housing bubble caused massive amounts of heartache. Unemployment went from five percent to ten percent and didn't get back down to five until 2015. The average American's income went down drastically, not returning to its pre-recession level until 2016—eight years after the bubble burst. Was there anything we could do about any of that? Nothing. Not one thing. We, and every other American, were victims of conditions we didn't create and couldn't control.

Now, I don't have any statistics, but I'm guessing that prescriptions for depression medication skyrocketed. One thing I'm certain of is that people got scared—and we were scared along with them. Some of them panicked and, as you know, people in panic-mode make bad decisions. That's "playing the victim," letting the outside world control your mindset and dictating your actions—or, better said, causing knee-jerk reactions. That's a choice, and the worst one you can make.

We couldn't control the economy or my industry, but there was one thing we knew we could control, our mindset. We worried but we did not panic. We made decisions proactively, not reactively.

Every day, Janiene concentrated all her attention on caring for this new little life placed in her trust and on taking care of our family. She focused on the positive steps we could take to move forward and not on the chaos of all those "the world is about to end" prophecies. Each day, a bit exhausted but with a full heart, she smiled. She'd share stories with me telling me why she smiled so much or laughed out loud that day.

Well, that initial one-year plan turned into five years, and later included another little one, Laurel. It only ended because that family moved to San Antonio. By then, they'd become, and remain to this day, our second family.

Even in the chaos of something like the Great Recession, you can move forward with intention instead of sitting and waiting for change or running to do something, anything! Living with intention brought a little financial support for the short term, but it also brought a wonderful, long-term connection with another family that will last a lifetime. Watching how my wife handled a situation that destroyed many families is just one more reason I feel like I hit the lottery when I married my wife.

She agrees.

You Control your Future.

Janiene's childhood was hugely different from mine. Her family foundation was not stable or predictable, as mine was. In her early twenties, she decided to take control of her life and move it in a different direction. It required a lot of effort. First, it required her to identify those unhealthy behaviors she'd learned and now needed to unlearn—things she did not want to repeat in her future family. This required her to look at herself with as much objectivity as possible, and without excuses, facing some harsh realities.

It goes without saying that you can't fix a problem unless you know what it is and, you need to know the difference between symptoms of the problem and the root of the problem itself. Janiene was determined to see herself as she was and get to the root of it. Only then did she take action. She started with counseling and the work that came with it. Lots of reading, lots of writing, lots of unraveling, and lots of sadness. It isn't an easy thing to watch someone go through this process, and my emotions frequently swung from feeling helpless to being immensely proud of her.

She was determined to find a positive and peaceful way to live. Something she had never really experienced growing up. Ultimately, she found it and that effort made her more than the amazing wife and mother she is today. It also made her the go-to person for family and friends in need of extra support or counsel, and a mentor to several young people in our school district.

One in particular, Neveah, has been Janiene's protégé since she was in sixth grade. That young woman will graduate from college next year. Janiene made the conscious choice in her early twenties to stop being a woman of anger and rage—a victim of her circumstances. She did the work and became a resource to others, a woman of empathy and wisdom for anyone who may need it, instead of one filled with anger and victimism. She ceased being a reactive personality and took proactive control of her future. In the process, she also created generational change for our family.

That's one of the many reasons my wife is a hero to me.

Always Start with the End in Mind

As you've guessed, I'm enormously proud of my son's baseball success. If you spoke to the 6-year-old Cam or 16-year-old Cam and asked him what he wanted to do when he grew up, the answer would have been the same: "I'm going to play professional baseball." Cam set a goal to play college baseball when he started high school and, every day, his purpose was to qualify—athletically and academically, to do so.

At the end of his first year playing, Cam came to me with a new line of thinking. Realizing the odds of playing professionally were incredibly remote. He said he understood his grade point average was now more important than his batting average. He said he'd checked the box marked "college athlete" and now planned to dedicate that same work ethic to academics, focusing on differentiating himself as a student and eventual professional.

He transferred to the University of Texas at Dallas where he studied business. He put his competitive energy towards something he felt would differentiate himself from his peers when entering the working world—sales.

Within two semesters, he ranked as the number two collegiate seller in the country. He even coached his school's national sales teams, raising the program to Top 3 nationally. This, however, was only an intermediate goal—a steppingstone in his long-range plan.

As Cam entered his senior year, he realized there was probably a significant difference between the classroom and the office. To continue his professional development, he joined one of the largest tech organizations in the world. Its development program had an industry-leading reputation which Cam found to be well-deserved. Today, Cam is 28 and six years into his post-graduate career. After four years in that first position, Cam decided he was ready for the next step in his plan. He moved to the company and role that he envisioned for himself when he was 19. He's happy at the new company, in large measure because he made the Top 1 percent Club both years.

He credits the clarity of his freshman vision and the successful completion of his intermediate goals as the (not-so-secret) secrets to his success.

Always be Looking for Talented People

In real estate, I learned early not to hire experienced agents. Most of those who wanted to join a team wanted it because they'd developed unhealthy habits that made them unsuccessful as independent agents.

Instead, I recruited the best talent I could find in other industries and taught them how to excel in my field. Amazing people will thrive when given great coaching, average people may improve, but will never be exceptional. The potential for exceptional must already be inside them when they're hired. Leaders can then provide them with the tools to be amazing but they have to use those tools properly to excel.

For example, Cecilia, who runs my office, left her old job 10 years ago and, on finding out, I immediately called and hired her, even though I didn't really have the need at the time. I knew her to be an incredibly selfless person, whose life had been spent achieving success at everything she attempted, regardless of the challenges.

She came to the US with her family from Vietnam just before high school and spoke no English. She had to spend the first year at home, watching TV and reading the dictionary in order to learn enough English to attend school. Four years later, she graduated as valedictorian. Next, she went on to play Division 1 soccer in college despite having a heart issue that required her to have a pacemaker implanted at age 18.

After completing an MBA from the University of Texas, she set up a charity where she made regular trips to Cambodia to rescue kids from child sex trafficking—at incredibly high risk to herself and those who came with her. She is also an amazing wife and mother to a young man who, because of the way she and her husband have raised him, will likely achieve as much or more than she has.

As a business owner or manager, when you know someone like Cecilia, you stand ready to hire them at the earliest opportunity. Even if a position doesn't exist at that moment, that person will be profitable to you in the long run. Cecilia has become a priceless part of my business success, as I knew she would.

Be the Leader Others Emulate

You can see lots of different styles of leadership just by looking at different coaches in sports and how they operate. For me, the best form of leadership is exemplary—doing things in such a way that those around you strive to be like you.

This is the type of leader I've been fortunate to have as my father, and the type of leadership I have aspired to instill in my own children.

When my daughter Kailey was in high school, she took a path that set her apart from many of her peers. While others indulged in drinking, drug use, and partying, Kailey chose to abstain. This decision, though challenging and often isolating, was a testament to a quieter, less glamorous form of leadership. It's easy to admire the bold leader who stands at the forefront, but true leadership sometimes requires standing firm in your values, even if it means standing alone. Kailey knew that being a leader meant staying true to herself even when it was inconvenient. Despite the pressures, she remained strong in her faith and core values. It wasn't until years after her high school graduation that she fully grasped the impact of her choices.

One day, out of the blue, she received a phone call from a high school friend she hadn't heard from in the five years since graduation. During that phone call, her friend opened up about a tough situation she was facing. A family member had just received a chilling medical diagnosis, and it threw her into a deep struggle with her faith. She felt angry with God and turned to substance abuse as a way to cope with her overwhelming emotions.

Even though they hadn't been in touch for years, that young woman immediately thought of Kailey when she hit rock bottom. It wasn't just about their past friendship; it was clear that Kailey's strong values and faith had left a lasting impression. When she needed support, prayer, and someone to help her navigate through her struggles, Kailey was the first person she thought to reach out to. This highlighted two particularly important aspects of Kailey's leadership:

Even though Kailey stood alone in her beliefs, her discipline did not go unnoticed. Her peers were aware that she chose not to partake in their activities, but they still saw her as a refuge—a judgment-free source of guidance and support. Her steadfast commitment to her principles made her a trusted confidante.

Kailey's leadership involved more than setting an example. It fostered an environment where individuals feel supported in their journey regardless of their missteps. By living authentically, Kailey unknowingly created that safe space where people could "fail forward" and with her help, meet their challenges and grow from those experiences. She made such a lasting impact that I'm sure she inspired others to follow in her footsteps.

Strong leaders lead by example and leave a lasting impact.

Perfect Balance is Impossible, your unimaginable life is not

The life I've led is far beyond my wildest expectations. I don't just say that about the material things—although having a 1300 square foot gym in my backyard is pretty awesome! I mean a life with no regrets—an intentional life where I got to determine the outcomes, rather than having to take what was handed to me. Being intentional about the things I believed to be most important in my life has given me a balance that allows me to wake up each day feeling not just grateful, but truly happy. When there are challenges in one area of my life, I'm supported by others that allow me to better deal with the challenges.

Striving for perfection is a recipe for disappointment, but being intentional about improving is your path to a life that otherwise may not be available to you. That's not to say you will have a perfect life (whatever that is), but rather to encourage you to follow these steps to have an intentional life one that will likely far surpass what you believed possible. A life where the baggage you've carried in your past is released and replaced with the life you now know is possible.

Though the time you spend on each piece of your Life Pie will vary greatly, the end results and ability to hit your goals for each will not. Like so many of the people I coach, you will be amazed at the differences made with the smallest efforts. From relationships, to finances, adventures/vacations, health goals, spiritual connection, and anything else you deem to be important in your life, **you can make them better**. And as you update your Life Pie each year, those areas will have new goals and experience new growth—growth you create, and growth that leads you to your unimaginable life. The changes made in the first year will impress you, but the improvements you continue to make year after year will change you. Though we will all live vastly different lives, the improvement we can make in those lives is within our control and is consistent for all of us.

Just as I discovered early on in my career, starting with the end in mind doesn't just help you achieve success in your work. It's the roadmap for success in life. Just think—your current life of hoping for a positive outcome in important areas of your life can be replaced with a future where you are strategic. By setting goals, you determine your outcomes and enjoy an amazing journey along the way.

The 80 Percent Project's Mission Statement

We teach people that work is not life; it is one part of life.
To be the best it can be, life must be balanced among personal,
family, and other aspects.
Achieving high-level success doesn't require the sacrifice of
everything else.

You can't achieve your best success at any aspect without success in all aspects.

My wife and I have lived this vision and created our unimaginable life. Now, we're watching our children live it and, by their example, help others live it.

We'd like to help you, too.

Ready to Dive In?

Here's What to Do to Get Started...
Your journey with *The 80 Percent Project* starts now!
We've got a free Life Pie waiting just for you—a simple
tool to help you visualize the key areas of your life.

Scan the QR code below to download your Life Pie

Fill it out and start making a difference!

Join our community of fellow 80 Percenters
for tips, support, and regular advice
straight from Andy himself.

Don't wait—take the first step toward the
life you deserve TODAY!

About the Author

Andy Allen

For over three decades, Andy has been instrumental in helping buyers, sellers, and agents reach their real estate goals. Ranked as high as #15 in the nation by *The Wall Street Journal*, Andy's team is a testament to his exceptional ability to empower agents to achieve their full potential. His commitment to excellence in real estate has always been balanced by a rich personal life.

Andy has developed innovative sales training programs that drive outstanding results while fostering a well-rounded, fulfilling lifestyle. His unwavering belief that "anything is possible" has inspired many of his former team members to build their own award-winning teams. Through disciplined practices and strategic insights, Andy has cultivated a life and career beyond what he once imagined.

Now, with a wealth of experience and achievements, Andy is dedicated to guiding others on how a successful career can complement a life well lived.

Website: https://www.my80percentproject.com/
LinkedIn: https://www.linkedin.com/in/andyallenaustintx/

Made in the USA
Columbia, SC
15 August 2025

8f965126-66d9-45c5-b9ba-f64151775a0aR01